Principles for Effective Pedagogy

The UK Teaching and Learning Research Programme (TLRP) worked for ten years to improve outcomes for learners in schools and other sectors through high quality research. One outcome of individual projects and across-Programme thematic work was the development of ten 'evidence-informed' principles for effective pedagogy. Synopses of these principles have been widely disseminated, particularly to practitioners. However, the evidence and reasoning underpinning them has not yet been fully explained. This book fills this gap by providing a scholarly account of the research evidence that informed the development of these principles, as well as offering some evidence of early take-up and impact. It also includes responses from highly-respected researchers throughout the world in order to locate the work in the broader international literature, to extend it by drawing on similar work elsewhere, to provide critique and to stimulate further development and debate. *Principles for Effective Pedagogy* contributes to international dialogue on effective teaching and learning, providing a focus for scholarly comment, sharing of expertise and knowledge accumulation.

This book was originally published as a special issue of *Research Papers in Education*.

Mary James, AcSS, is part-time Associate Director of Research at the University of Cambridge Faculty of Education. She is President of the British Educational Research Association (2011–13). She was a long time member of the Assessment Reform Group and founding editor of *The Curriculum Journal*. From 2002–07 she was Deputy Director of the ESRC Teaching and Learning Research Programme, and she subsequently held an ESRC Programme Director's Fellowship. At the same time she was Director of a major TLRP project on 'Learning How to Learn in classrooms, schools and networks'.

Andrew Pollard, AcSS, was Director of the Teaching and Learning Research Programme from 2002–09 and Chair of the UK's Strategic Forum for Research in Education from 2008–10. He is a former school teacher and his research interests include teaching-learning processes, learner perspectives and the development of evidence-informed classroom practice. He has worked extensively on the effects of national and institutional policies on learning and has directed longitudinal studies on the impact of education legislation on primary school classrooms and on pupil experience and learning from age 4–16.

Principles for Effective Pedagogy

International responses to evidence from the
UK Teaching & Learning Research Programme

Edited by
Mary James and Andrew Pollard

Routledge
Taylor & Francis Group

LONDON AND NEW YORK

First published 2012
by Routledge
2 Park Square, Milton Park, Abingdon, Oxon, OX14 4RN

Simultaneously published in the USA and Canada
by Routledge
711 Third Avenue, New York, NY 10017

Routledge is an imprint of the Taylor & Francis Group, an informa business

This book is a reproduction of *Research Papers in Education*, volume 26, issue 3. The Publisher requests to those authors who may be citing this book to state, also, the bibliographical details of the special issue on which the book was based.

Trademark notice: Product or corporate names may be trademarks or registered trademarks, and are used only for identification and explanation without intent to infringe.

British Library Cataloguing in Publication Data
A catalogue record for this book is available from the British Library

ISBN13: 978-0-415-67662-5

Typeset in Times New Roman
by Taylor & Francis Books

Disclaimer
The publisher would like to make readers aware that the chapters in this book are referred to as articles as they had been in the special issue. The publisher accepts responsibility for any inconsistencies that may have arisen in the course of preparing this volume for print.

Contents

Notes on Contributors

Tadahiko Abiko is Professor of Curriculum Studies, Graduate School of Teacher Education, Waseda University, Japan. He graduated from the University of Tokyo and was awarded an MA from the University of Tokyo and a PhD from Nagoya University. He was co-founder and former Executive Director of the Japanese Society for Curriculum Studies. He has been an ordinary member of the Central Council for Education in the Ministry of Education, Culture, Sports, Science and Technology since 2005. His speciality is curriculum development, particularly of lower secondary schools, including curriculum evaluation and instructional methods. Since 2002, he has been an overseas corresponding editor of *The Curriculum Journal*.

Linda Allal obtained a PhD in Educational Psychology at Michigan State University. After a career spanning 30 years as Professor in the Faculty of Psychology and Educational Sciences of the University of Geneva, she is Professor Emerita since 2006. Her research and publications focus on the relations between learning, teaching and assessment in classroom settings. Author of numerous articles and book chapters, her recent publications include a book, co-edited with L. Mottier Lopez, on the regulation of learning in the classroom and in teacher training (*Régulation des apprentissages en situation scolaire et en formation,* De Boeck, 2007) and a volume, co-edited with L. Lafortune, on teachers' professional judgement in their practice of classroom assessment *(Jugement professionnel en évaluation*, Presses de l'Université du Québec, 2008).

Marlies Baeten is a PhD student at the Centre for Research on Professional Learning, Development, Corporate Training and Lifelong Learning, University of Leuven, Belgium. Her research interests lie in the field of student-centred teaching and learning in higher education. She is particularly interested in students' perceptions and their approaches to learning in student-centred learning environments.

Inneke Berghmans is a PhD student at the Centre for Research on Professional Learning, Development, Corporate Training and Lifelong Learning, University of Leuven, Belgium. Her research focuses on Peer Assisted Learning within the field of higher education, especially approaches to peer tutoring and their effects on students' learning.

Filip Dochy, PhD, is Professor of Research on Learning, Training and Development at the Centre for Research on Professional Learning, Development, Corporate Training and Lifelong Learning, University of Leuven, Belgium. His research interest is in assessment, learning and development, cooperative and team learning. He is a member of the Executive Committee of EARLI (European Association for Research on Learning and Instruction), and he is chair of the Board of EAPRIL (European Association for Practitioner Research on Improving Learning in Education and the Professions). He is founding editor of the *Educational Research Review.*

Lorna Earl, PhD, is a Director, Aporia Consulting Ltd. and the current President of the International Congress of School Effectiveness and School Improvement. She recently retired from a position as Associate Professor in the Theory and Policy Studies Department and Head of the International Centre for Educational Change at OISE/UT and is currently a part-time Professor at the University of Auckland. Lorna has worked for over 20 years in schools, school boards, ministries of education and universities. As a leader in the field of assessment and evaluation, she has been involved in consultation, research, evaluation and staff development with teachers' organisations, ministries of education, school boards and charitable foundations in Canada, England, Australia, New Zealand, Europe and the United States. She is a prolific author and has written books, chapters and articles about assessment, using data for decision-making, evaluation methods, knowledge mobilisation and networking for school improvement.

Ingrid Gogolin is a Professor for International Comparative and Multicultural Education Research at the University of Hamburg. She has served as President of the German and the European Educational Research Associations. Her main research areas are as follows: international comparison of education systems; migration, multilingualism, linguistic diversity and their consequences for education; historical development of national educational systems, their linguistic habitus, and the role and function of national languages for education.

David Hogan is currently Professor and Principal Research Scientist, National Institute of Education, Singapore. Prior to that, Professor Hogan was Dean, Office of Education Research at NIE (2008–2010) and before that Dean of the Centre for Research of Pedagogy and Practice (CRPP) at NIE (2005–2008), and Vice Dean for Research and Methodology at CRPP/ NIE (2004–2005). Before joining NIE, Professor Hogan was Professor of Education at the University of Tasmania in Hobart (1994–2004). Between 1979 and 1993, he was first assistant and then an Associate Professor at the University of Pennsylvania in Philadelphia, Pennsylvania. His research interests currently focus on measuring, mapping and modelling classroom instruction and its impact on student learning, broadly conceived, and the design and implementation of large-scale reform initiatives.

Mary James is Professor and Associate Director of Research at the University of Cambridge Faculty of Education. She is President of the British Educational Research. With Andrew Pollard, she is the member of Expert Panel appointed by the Department of Education in England to review the National Curriculum. From 2005 to 2008 she held a Chair of Education at the Institute of Education, University of London, where she was Deputy Director of the Economic and Social Research Council's Teaching and Learning Research Programme, with responsibility for supporting school-based projects. She was the Director of one of the largest TLRP projects: 'Learning How to Learn in classrooms, schools and networks'. In 2008 she also held an ESRC Programme Director's Fellowship. She was a member of the UK

Assessment Reform Group from 1992 to 2010, and advised the Curriculum Development Institute, of the Hong Kong Government's Education Bureau during its 10-year period of educational reform. She began her working life with 10 years as a secondary school teacher.

Eva Kyndt, PhD, is a Postdoctoral Researcher at the Centre for Research on Professional Learning, Development, Corporate Training and Lifelong Learning, University of Leuven, Belgium. She is assistant editor of the *Educational Research Review*. Her research interests are approaches to learning, professional learning, informal learning and learning climate. She investigates these topics in both educational and professional settings.

Andrew Pollard is Professor of Education at the Department of Quantitative Social Science, Institute of Education, University of London, where he supports research impact. He is Director of ESCalate, the Education Subject Centre of the UK's Higher Education Academy at the University of Bristol. He chairs the Education Sub-panel for the 2004 Research Excellence Framework on behalf of UK Higher Education Funding Councils. With Mary James, he is a member of the Expert Panel appointed by the Department for Education in England to review the National Curriculum. He was Director of the ESRC's Teaching and Learning Research Programme from 2002 to 2009 and held an ESRC Programme Director's Fellowship in 2010. He was also Director of the UK Strategic Forum for Research in Education from 2008 to 2011. He is responsible for a popular textbook and support materials on reflective teaching within primary and secondary schooling. His early research developed into the Identify and Learning Programme (ILP), a longitudinal ethnographic study of the interaction of identify, learning, assessment, career and social differentiation in children's experiences of schooling from age 4 to 16. He began his career as a primary school teacher.

Introduction

Between 2002 and 2009, we were involved in coordinating the largest programme of educational research on teaching and learning that the UK has ever seen. Involving around 700 researchers in some 100 project and thematic investments spread over about ten years, the Economic and Social Research Council's Teaching and Learning Research Programme (TLRP) investigated ways to improve outcomes for learners at all ages and stages in all sectors and contexts of education and training. Research on teaching and learning processes and the implications for teachers' professional learning was at the heart of this.

By 2006, we began to look across the 22 school-based projects that completed early in the Programme to see if there were any general insights emerging about effective pedagogy.In later years, we also considered analyses arising from TLRP research in further education, higher education and lifelong learning – though, to reduce complexity, we have not drawn substantively on this work here.

In recent years the word 'pedagogy' had been shunned in England, either because it was regarded as jargon or because, literally speaking, it only refers to the learning of children and not adults. However, this is changing and politicians as well as education professionals are becoming more comfortable with the term applied to learning and teaching at all ages. This is important because what 'pedagogy' does is recognise the fundamental interactions between teaching and learning in formal settings. They are not separate processes but are contingent upon each other: learning follows teaching, and teaching follows learning.

The concept of 'pedagogy' recognises that there are some basic and fundamental understandings (or principles) about learning and teaching that can be 'known' and that this knowledge base can provide teachers with practical ideas that they can apply, test, adapt and develop according to the demands of the contexts in which they work. In so doing, teachers create new knowledge of 'principles in practice' and potentially contribute to the practical knowledge base themselves. This demands that teachers reflect in, and on, action and critique and share their understandings. It offers them opportunities for an enhanced professionalism that can be far more rewarding, for all concerned, than simply 'delivering' under-theorised prescribed practices.

The position of TLRP was that a great deal is known about effective pedagogy, both in the UK and internationally, but the synthesis, communication, implementation and embedding of such knowledge had been far weaker than it should be. This was one of the reasons why, in attempting to draw together some of the key findings of schools projects, we chose to present them in the form of ten principles for effective teaching and learning (see the list at the end of this Introduction). We published them first in a TLRP Commentary (a short, accessible discussion document) then refined them in a Guide for Teachers with illustrative evidence. Using these vehicles, we invited practitioners and policymakers to consider how a limited number of key principles, derived from well-founded research evidence and scholarship, might engage professionals and support them in making contextualised judgements, whilst, at the same time, progressively generating understanding and a language for use in a renewed public debate about the why, what and how of future education policy.

This collection focuses on the second purpose: to help stimulate renewed public debate about pedagogy and its implications for policy and practice. We wanted particularly to draw in researchers, from across the world, who are working on similar questions but in different contexts. This, we judged, would enable discussion about definitions of key concepts, methods for researching effective practice, evidence of process and outcomes, validity of different perspectives and interpretations, and issues in knowledge management, dissemination and use. We have not been disappointed.

We hope the initial review in this collection, which sets out the rationale, development, evidence, argument and impact of TLRP's ten principles for effective pedagogy, together with the six responses from continental Europe, Asian Pacific countries and North America, will together provide a rich resource for further deliberation, debate and the extension of knowledge and understanding.

We might have presented the contributions in a variety of ways, but we chose, quite simply, to start with those from Europe, geographically proximal to the UK, followed by the two from East and South-East Asia, both 'high-performing jurisdictions', concluding with the piece from Canada. As it happens, the first contributions focus closely on the phenomenon of pedagogy and related concepts, whilst later contributions shift focus somewhat onto considerations concerning the strengths and weaknesses of research centres and programmes as vehicles for knowledge generation and utilisation.

Linda Allal's commentary is contextualised in the French-speaking academic community and is helpful in making comparisons by drawing on literature of which most Anglophone researchers have limited awareness. She presents an argument for retaining the term 'teaching and learning' in favour of pedagogy in order to keep the focus on the learning rather than teaching, which has been a pre-occupation in Francophone countries. She regards a concern with teaching–learning transactions and learning outcomes to be a strength of the British tradition. There is also a strong and valuable focus on theoretical and methodological frameworks in this contribution.

Ingrid Gogolin's commentary provides an extensive contextual comparison with German teaching and learning research and addresses fundamental values concerning the position of the learner. Particularly interesting are reactions to the shockwaves from the 2001 PISA results, which reverberate still. Germany, according to this account, woke up to the need to consider what students actually learned as a result of teaching, because outcomes could not be assumed. Gogolin also raises the challenging issue of whether TLRP (and other English-speaking) researchers might be encouraged to submit their work to non-English journals so that the research becomes better known across Europe.

The commentary from Filip Dochy and colleagues helpfully draws out, from psychological and social-psychological perspectives, some contradictions in the evidence on what constitutes effective pedagogy. They argue for a balanced view that values both individual and social learning and direct instruction as well as co-construction. Their work is mainly in post-school contexts where informal learning features prominently.

Tadahiko Abiko provides another interesting comparative perspective on the principles. He is particularly interesting on the role of sociology of education in Japan, which is often overlooked by writers who research teaching and learning from a predominantly psychological perspective. Some readers will undoubtedly find Abiko's demystification of 'lesson study', which originated in Japan but which has now spread worldwide, to be particularly illuminating.

David Hogan's commentary, from Singapore, whilst critical of our analysis, concludes rather positively. Hogan affirms the resonance of the ten principles but suggests that decision-making, at either classroom or government level, requires a deeper, more integrative framework. He also makes an interesting comparison of the relative advantages of more tightly controlled research centres, as the one he directs, with more loosely coupled research programmes, as TLRP was.

Lorna Earl, from Canada, chose to focus on two rather different issues, but both close to her own interests – knowledge management and assessment for learning. Particularly in relation to user engagement and knowledge management, she extends her analysis beyond the theme of pedagogy and provides a commentary on the strategic efforts that TLRP made to have genuine impact on all those individuals and communities that might benefit from its work.

Underpinning all these commentaries are a number of recurring themes, which we hope will stimulate lively debate and further research. Many imply a consideration of appropriate balance and relationships, for example: between a focus on teaching and a focus on learning; between transactions and outcomes; between learning tasks and other activities; between the individual learner and the group; between commonality and difference; between psychological and sociological perspectives; between experimental and other research designs; between knowledge management and knowledge utilisation; between centres and programmes as effective infrastructures for productive research.

Acknowledgements

In writing this Introduction, our thanks go especially to Alan Brown and Judy Sebba who read all the commentaries and offered us valuable insights on the contributions that each made to the whole.

Appendix

TLRP's ten principles for effective pedagogy

1. Effective pedagogy equips learners for life in its broadest sense. Learning should aim to help individuals and groups to develop the intellectual, personal and social resources that will enable them to participate as active citizens, contribute to economic development and flourish as individuals in a diverse and changing society. This means adopting a broad conception of worthwhile learning outcomes and taking seriously issues of equity and social justice for all.

2. Effective pedagogy engages with valued forms of knowledge. Pedagogy should engage learners with the big ideas, key skills and processes, modes of discourse, ways of thinking and practising, attitudes and relationships, which are the most valued learning processes and outcomes in particular contexts. They need to understand what constitutes quality, standards and expertise in different settings.

3. Effective pedagogy recognises the importance of prior experience and learning. Pedagogy should take account of what the learner knows already in order for them, and those who support their learning, to plan their next steps. This includes building on prior learning but also taking account of the personal and cultural experiences of different groups of learners.

4. Effective pedagogy requires learning to be scaffolded. Teachers, trainers and all those, including peers, who support the learning of others should provide activities, cultures and structures of intellectual, social and emotional support to help learners to move forward in their learning. When these supports are removed, the learning needs to be secure.

5. Effective pedagogy needs assessment to be congruent with learning. Assessment should be designed and implemented with the goal of achieving maximum validity both in terms of learning outcomes and learning processes. It should help to advance learning as well as determine whether learning has occurred.

6. Effective pedagogy promotes the active engagement of the learner. A chief goal of learning should be the promotion of learners' independence and autonomy. This involves acquiring a repertoire of learning strategies and practices, developing positive learning dispositions and having the will and confidence to become agents in their own learning.

7. Effective pedagogy fosters both individual and social processes and outcomes. Learners should be encouraged and helped to build relationships and communication with others for learning purposes, in order to assist the mutual construction of knowledge and enhance the achievements of individuals and groups. Consulting learners about their learning and giving them a voice is both an expectation and a right.

8. Effective pedagogy recognises the significance of informal learning. Informal learning, such as learning out of school or away from the workplace, should be recognised as at least as significant as formal learning and should therefore be valued and appropriately utilised in formal processes.

9. Effective pedagogy depends on the learning of all those who support the learning of others. The need for lecturers, teachers, trainers and co-workers to learn continuously in order to develop their knowledge and skill, and adapt and develop their roles, especially through practice-based inquiry, should be recognised and supported.

10. Effective pedagogy demands consistent policy frameworks with support for learning as their primary focus. Organisational and system-level policies need to recognise the fundamental importance of continual learning – for individual, team, organisational and system success – and be designed to create effective learning environments for all learners.

Mary James
Faculty of Education
University of Cambridge, UK
mej1002@cam.ac.uk

Andrew Pollard
Institute of Education
University of London, UK

TLRP's ten principles for effective pedagogy: rationale, development, evidence, argument and impact

Mary James[a] and Andrew Pollard[b]

[a]Faculty of Education, University of Cambridge, UK; [b]Department of Quantitative Social Science, Institute of Education, University of London, UK

The ESRC Teaching and Learning Research Programme (TLRP) worked for ten years to improve outcomes for learners across the United Kingdom. Individual projects within the Programme focused on different research questions and utilised a range of methods and theoretical resources. Across-programme thematic seminar series and task groups enabled emerging findings to be analysed, synthesised and communicated to wider audiences. One outcome of this activity was the development of ten 'evidence-informed' principles, which engaged with diverse forms of evidence, whilst acknowledging that 'users' would need to judge how best to implement such principles in their particular contexts. Synopses of these principles were published in posters and booklets, from 2006, but the evidence and reasoning underpinning them has not been fully explained. This contribution attempts to fill this gap. It provides a justification for the production of the TLRP principles and describes the iterative process by which they were developed. It clusters the ten principles in four broad areas that reflect the multilayered nature of innovation in pedagogy: (1) educational values and purposes; (2) curriculum, pedagogy and assessment; (3) personal and social processes and relationships; and (4) teachers and policies. It elaborates the argument and evidence for each principle, drawing not only on findings from projects but, crucially, the thematic initiatives that began the synthetic work. There is also an attempt, though by no means comprehensive, to relate TLRP insights to research and scholarship beyond the Programme's school-focused work in order to ground them in a wider literature: to work in other sectors of education; and to the broader literature that has accumulated internationally and over time. Finally, the five years since the principles were first published provides some evidence of impact. Although direct impact on learner outcomes cannot be measured, it is possible to provide an account of take-up by mediating agencies and others. The piece has been prepared as a contribution to international dialogue on effective teaching and learning and to provide a focus for scholarly comment, sharing of expertise and knowledge accumulation.

Rationale

The bold aim of the Teaching and Learning Research Programme (TLRP) was to work to improve outcomes for learners of all ages in teaching and learning contexts across the United Kingdom. At the conclusion of TLRP's work,[1] it is appropriate to consider what it has contributed to the understanding and advancement of effective pedagogy.

What is meant by 'effective pedagogy'?

The effectiveness of educational provision needs to be evaluated by reference to the goals and values of the society it serves. Within contemporary Western democracies, three major strands of philosophical and political thinking on educational purposes are well established. The first concerns teaching and learning linked to *economic productivity* – and has taken various forms historically as labour market needs have evolved. The second concerns *social cohesion* and the inclusion (or control) of different groups within society – this remains important within our unequal and diverse communities today. The third concerns *personal development*, fulfilment and expression – with a contemporary manifestation perhaps in the term 'wellbeing'. The three are, of course, deeply interconnected. Indeed, the view taken here conceptualises 'effectiveness' as a mutually beneficial synergy among the three.

What then of 'pedagogy'? Many years ago, Simon published a paper entitled: 'Why no pedagogy in England?' (1981). He compared the multi-disciplinary and scientific tradition of pedagogic thought and practice in Europe with the more instrumental approach to teaching that he found in England. Here, he argued, the development of teaching was dominated by a concern with the individual differences between learners and groups of learners, and how to respond to them. In contrast, as Simon put it:

> To develop effective pedagogy means starting from the opposite standpoint, from what children have in common as members of the human species; to establish the general principles of teaching and, in the light of these, to determine what modifications of practice are necessary to meet specific individual needs. (131)

This argument can be chased through at two main levels. It has implications for forms of institutional provision – and Simon was a strong supporter of the comprehensive principle. It also has implications for teaching and learning practices and the way the highly contentious phrase, 'what works', is understood.

The TLRP, which has supported more than 100 projects, fellowships, thematic groups and capacity-building initiatives, focused primarily on the second of these two levels: on teaching and learning in authentic settings inside and outside of schools and other institutions, through the life course. The specific findings of TLRP's projects are described in research briefings, articles, books, websites and other media. Its cross-programme thematic work is published in a series of commentaries on contemporary policy issues, as well as in special issues of journals, research reviews for external bodies, and in briefing papers for direct communications with policy makers.[2]

A major ambition of the Programme, for both analytic and impact purposes, has been to try to produce an evidence-informed statement of 'general principles' of teaching and learning, just as Simon advocated. The basic view is that a great deal is actually known about pedagogy, both in the UK and internationally, but that the synthesis, communication and implementation of such knowledge are far weaker than they should be.

Why general 'principles' are an important outcome of TLRP

The diverse nature of TLRP's projects, which focused on different research questions in different contexts, sometimes using different methods and theoretical perspectives, did not permit formal quantitative meta-analysis rendering aggregated effect sizes of interventions as indicators of 'what works'. However, each project engaged with existing research in its own particular field or sub-field and built on this to take knowledge forward cumulatively. Through the mechanisms for knowledge exchange set up by TLRP, and drawing on their own particular networks and resources, research teams also developed thinking in dialogue with other researchers and users. In this way new insights were located in intellectual and political context through social processes.[3]

The expectation that the research would be carried out in authentic settings made it impossible to control all the variables operating at any one time. But it enabled researchers, working with practitioners, to grapple with the issues of implementation that so often confound best efforts to 'scale up' promising innovations. Furthermore, it enabled practitioners to use their knowledge, of the features of particular settings and characteristics of learners, to develop and refine generalisations from the original research.

For all these reasons, when TLRP was asked what it (as a Programme) had found out about effective teaching and learning, generally, it was not justifiable to make unequivocal claims about findings in terms of categorical knowledge or cause–effect relationships. However, it was possible, in our judgement, to offer 'evidence-informed principles', which could engage with diverse forms of evidence whilst calling for the necessary application of contextualised judgement by teachers, practitioners and/or policy makers. Such principles, we believed, could enable the accumulation and organisation of knowledge in resilient, realistic and practically useful ways, and had the potential, progressively, to generate understanding and language for use within public debates.

How the ten principles were developed

The analytical and synthetic approach to reviewing the TLRP evidence involved an iterative process of working between the conceptual map that TLRP had developed to represent the scope of its interests with reference to teaching and learning (see Figure 1), and the outputs that were beginning to emerge from individual TLRP projects and cross-Programme thematic work. This model had a long gestation and can, in an early form, be found in a sociological analysis of classroom coping strategies (Pollard 1982). However, it was simplified to its key elements to provide an analytic framework to structure cross-Programme discussion and analysis.

The majority of projects that were funded in the early phases of TLRP commissioning were focused on the school sector and these were considered first.[4] However, many of the thematic initiatives went wider than the school sector. These were attempts to review findings across TLRP in relation to specific key ideas[5] and to relate these insights to research and scholarship beyond TLRP in order to ground them in a wider literature. This review has a similar ambition: to provide a synoptic overview of what TLRP's schools projects discovered about effective pedagogy but to relate this to TLRP's work in other sectors of education, and to the broader literature that has accumulated internationally and over time. This is a grand ambition and has necessitated selection and précis in order to produce an accessible digest.

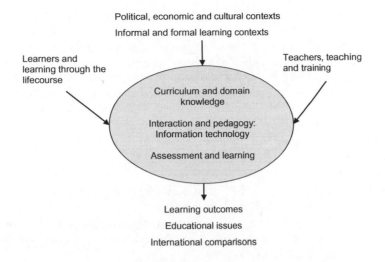

Figure 1. The conceptual scope of TLRP's interests relevant to pedagogy.

The schools projects and the thematic work reviewed here are listed in the Appendix. The codes allocated to such projects (P1–P21) and to thematic work (T1–T17) are used as a referencing system, unless a particular output needs to be cited. Other publications are accessible by following the web links given in the Appendix. Other TLRP investments are sometimes also referred to using standard referencing conventions and are not listed in the appendix. All TLRP work is accessible via www.tlrp.org.

The way in which the TLRP Directors' Team tackled the analytical and synthetic task is best described as 'narrative review'. One piece of thematic work (T12), led by Torrance and Sebba, was explicitly directed towards promoting a better understanding of the nature and roles of reviews of research. A typology of reviews was developed, which distinguished between reviews for academic and scholarly purposes and those for practice and policy purposes The iterative review that the TLRP carried out was intended to serve both sets of purposes and attempts to address multiple audiences, albeit in rather different forms of presentation – an example of 'commitment to "multi-vocalism" in review processes' (Torrance and Sebba 2007, 3).

In terms of the classification developed by this thematic group, the present contribution cannot claim to be either a 'definitive' review of the 'state of knowledge' in the whole field, or a 'systematic' review intended to produce 'conclusive, generalisable, politically defensible knowledge for action'. Although the evidence base is extensive, and reaches beyond TLRP, teaching and learning has too many dimensions for a single review to be definitive. Furthermore, evaluative exclusion and inclusion criteria were not strictly applied as expected in systematic reviews. In some senses this was not felt to be necessary because almost all the projects in TLRP's portfolio, funded in the 'generic phase' to 2009, were evaluated as 'Good' or 'Outstanding' by independent peer and user referees appointed by the ESRC.[6] The single exception was not criticised for the quality of its design, methods or analysis but because its outputs were rather thin at the time when the end of award report was submitted.[7]

Preliminary work on this narrative review, the explicit aim of which was to add value to the TLRP by synthesising its most important findings, was accelerated by the need in 2005 to respond to an invitation from the education team at HM Treasury, under the then Chancellor of the Exchequer, Gordon Brown, to brief it about the progress of TLRP research. Aware of the current policy push for 'rapid reviews' or 'rapid evidence appraisal' (Boaz, Solesbury, and Sullivan 2004), and the limited time to present an oral account of TLRP's work, the notion of ten principles offered a purposive framework for an initial summary of findings from projects just completing, and some suitably tentative implications for policy in the light of the recently published 2005 Budget Report.

A model for 'principles', as a valued output from research review, was already in the public domain: the UK Assessment Reform Group had used this format as a way of summarising the evidence on effective 'assessment for learning' (formative assessment) (ARG 2002). The ARG principles had been presented in a poster and disseminated widely by the Group and other organisations. Several years after publication these could still be found displayed in school classrooms and staffrooms, and used in the documentation of other agencies, although not always with clear attribution (see, e.g. DCSF 2008, 6).

The meeting at the Treasury convinced the TLRP Directors' Team of the need to publish something along similar lines for a general audience. So, in March 2006, it published *Improving teaching and learning in schools* as the second in its series of commentaries (James and Pollard 2006). Initially written in response to the Schools White Paper, which later became the Education and Inspections Act 2006, this commentary argued that no amount of structural reform, such as the creation of different types of schools, would obviate the need for serious attention to the quality of relationships and pedagogic processes in classroom if the standards of education were genuinely to improve. Included in the commentary was the first version of the TLRP's ten 'evidence-informed principles for effective teaching and learning', presented graphically on an ellipse to indicate that they represent no firm linear hierarchy. However, the sequence had a logic which helped with deciding an order when elaborated in text: beginning with pedagogical aims, and the way these are expressed in classroom practice, and extending to the conditions needed for effective pedagogy in the structures and cultures of schooling and the wider environment, including social and educational policy, locally and nationally. The relationship between elements was likened to the ripples when a pebble is thrown into a pond (James and Pollard 2006, 5).

Educational innovation, even that which is primarily classroom-focused, almost always involves changes at several levels, which makes researching it similarly multilayered. However, by examining the evidence against the categories, and the categories against the evidence, the themes of interest were eventually reduced to four main clusters (see James and Pollard 2008):

(1) educational values and purposes;
(2) curriculum, pedagogy and assessment;
(3) personal and social processes and relationships;
(4) teachers and policies.

TLRP's ten principles were grouped under these headings (as they are in the Evidence section below). In most publications they are described as principles of effective teaching and learning. But here, as indicated in the title of this contribution, the term pedagogy is preferred for four main reasons. First, the audience for this contribution will be familiar with the term and not regard it as academic jargon. Second, the term is now more widely used by UK practitioners and policy makers, and it is used across most sectors of education and training, which was not the case when TLRP was set up. Third, and most importantly, 'pedagogy' expresses the *contingent relationship* between teaching and learning (see the quotation from Simon above) and does not treat teaching as something that can be considered separately from an understanding of how learners learn. Fourth, as TLRP researchers themselves pointed out, the work of the programme, certainly as it pertained to schools, focused more clearly on the implications for teaching of what we know about learning, than it did on developing new knowledge about learning per se.

In an article reflecting further on the question that Brian Simon posed in 1981, Alexander (2004, 11) defines pedagogy as follows:

> Pedagogy is the act of teaching together with its attendant discourse. It is what one needs to know, and the skills one needs to command, in order to make and justify the many different kinds of decisions ofwhich teaching is constituted.

This fits very well with the way TLRP came to understand pedagogy, and the present task of setting out the empirical and theoretical justification for the principles that we distiled from the work of the Programme.

As noted earlier, the ten principles were first generated with school teaching and learning in mind, drawing primarily on evidence from the schools projects. This focus is reflected in this contribution. However, there was interest in other sectors and the TLRP Directors' Team was committed to exploring whether they might apply elsewhere. At the annual meeting for TLRP researchers, in November 2006, a session[8] was devoted to critique of the principles as currently formulated and to questioning whether they had relevance in the post-compulsory settings that many later-funded projects were researching. This generated a lot of discussion, but the idea of having a similar set of principles for other sectors was generally endorsed. As a consequence, the wording of the ten principles was amended to be more generic. Later they were developed in two further Commentaries: one on effective teaching and learning in UK higher education and the other on higher skills development in the workplace.[9] have also been built on in a handbook for practitioners (Pollard 2008) and in a further Commentary on professionalism and pedagogy (Pollard 2010).[10]

In the discussion that follows, this later version of the ten principles is used. There are two reasons for this decision. First, although contexts for learning vary, the common features in how people learn across the life course makes the validity of a shared set of principles sufficient to be worthy of serious consideration. Second, the majority of school projects had findings related to the importance of the learning of teachers as a condition for effective support of the learning of their pupils. Teachers are adult learners in the workplace and therefore the principles needed to apply to their learning too.

From 2005 to the present, discussions between researchers, practitioners, policy makers and other 'user' groups, have been a principal means of developing, refining and validating both the synthesis of research and the principles that arise from it. If these principles are valued as a way to accumulate and organise knowledge, with potential for further progressive development and use within public debates, then such discussion and iterative development will need to continue.

Argument and evidence

In this main section, the thinking underlying the articulation of particular principles is rehearsed and informing evidence from TLRP is outlined. The discussion is organised under the four headings given above. The aim is to identify the insights that TLRP researchers shared, and those on which they differed, and to tease out some of the underlying reasons for synergies or tensions. Some illustrative evidence from individual projects is included although projects or thematic initiatives, as entities, are more fully described elsewhere. Brief outlines are also available in audits of schools projects that have been written for other purposes (e.g. James and Pollard 2009; Pollard 2010).

Educational values and purposes (principle 1)

In the early days of the TLRP, a core objective was expressed as a need to investigate those teaching and learning practices that are most efficient and effective in enhancing the achievements of learners.[11] Given the policy context in the schools sector at the time, there was an assumption that projects would provide evidence of gains in pupil attainment. This created difficulties for some project teams. First, properly validated standard measures did not exist for some of the outcomes that projects had been funded to research, e.g. learning how to learn capability. Second, causal relationships were difficult to establish in authentic settings where variables interact in uncontrollable ways. Third, most research projects depended on the cooperation of teachers and sometimes it was difficult to convince them that, say, the link between pupil engagement and better attainment is not self-evident.

Many TLRP researchers also resisted taking for granted the idea that gains in pupil attainment on standard measures, such as national test or examination results, were necessarily 'a good thing'. They thought it important to examine the validity and reliability of these measures, to scrutinise the deeper purposes that such attainments were supposed to serve, and to investigate their effects on the behaviour of stakeholders. For example, were test results good indicators of enduring understanding and capability in important domains of learning? Did they lead to personal fulfilment and well-being? Did they contribute to the economic prosperity of the nation or to greater social justice and inclusion?

Some projects began to raise serious questions about the culture of performativity and/or the measures currently used (e.g. P7, P11, P13, P19, P21). In so doing, they rejected the notion that the responsibility of researchers is simply to report 'what works' in terms defined by others, especially groups who have strong vested interests. They pursued the idea that scholars and researchers have a legitimate role to play in democratic discussions about the aims, purposes and outcomes of education.

TLRP worked with the Philosophy of Education Society of Great Britain to examine the way in which the increasingly diverse intellectual resources of the educational research community might inform policy and, by extension, practice (T11). One paper from this thematic group (Bridges and Watts 2008) argues that policy demands a much wider range of information than empirical research typically provides. One of the gaps is the normative gap. The values that inform policy *can* be investigated empirically, but empirical investigation alone cannot tell us what we *ought* to do. However, other forms of disciplined enquiry can address these normative questions. As Bridges (2009, 3) summarises:

We should be more explicit about the educational and wider political values which frame policy and practice, and be more ready to subject these to careful scholarly, as well as democratic, scrutiny and criticism. The fact that ideology, normativity and educational values and principles are central to policy does not mean that scholarly endeavour has no work to do in these areas. The academy has enormous resources – in political science, social theory, ethics and philosophy – which can be brought to bear on this dimension of policy formation, and we should not be coy about using them.

Another thematic group (T2), which was convened earlier in the life of TLRP, examined how the first 30 projects to be funded (12 from the schools sector) used theoretical resources and empirical evidence to identify the learning outcomes of most interest in their specific context. Initial analysis of project documentation enabled seven categories of outcome to be identified:

(1) Attainments – often school curriculum based (literacy, numeracy, science) or measures of basic competence in the workplace.
(2) Understanding – of ideas, concepts, processes.
(3) Cognitive and creative – imaginative construction of meaning, arts or performance.
(4) Using – how to practise, manipulate, behave, engage in process or systems.
(5) Higher order learning – advanced thinking, reasoning, metacognition.
(6) Dispositions – attitudes, perceptions, motivations.
(7) Membership, inclusion, self-worth – affinity towards, and readiness to participate and contribute to, groups; building social and substantive identities. (James and Brown 2005, 11)

Box 1

Evidence from school projects

Many individual projects were interested in developing and researching achievements in several of these areas. For example, the Group Work projects (P6, P12) investigated motivation, attitudes, social–emotional relationships, and classroom behaviour as well as academic outcomes. The Thinking Skills project (P5) researched the broader learning goals of metacognition and self-regulation, and showed a positive relationship with academic attainment and effort, although the effect needed time to build and was not uniform across all learner groups (McGuinness et al. 2006). Similarly, the Learning How to Learn project (P13) investigated learning practices and strategies, alongside more conventional academic outcomes defined by national test results (James et al. 2007). In an early years project on learning and ICT (P1), enhanced learning dispositions and confidence were found to be crucial to building knowledge and skill (Stephen and Plowman 2008). The development of dispositions was also prominent in the longitudinal projects on the formation of learning identities (P21). And, two projects (P10, P15) investigated the benefits of consulting pupils in accordance with Article 12 of the United Nations Convention on the Rights of the Child, and in fulfilment of the aspirations for citizenship education through the practice of democratic values.

The evidence in Box 1 indicates that TLRP research and deliberation justified and embraced a wide definition of educational values, purposes and outcomes.

Attainments as measured by national tests and qualifications were by no means ignored but there was interest in other 'outcomes', such as engagement, participation, learning skills, dispositions and strategies, and the development of learning identities and autonomy. This range offered possibilities for a mutually productive synergy among educational aims linked to economic productivity, to the promotion of social cohesion and to personal flourishing. In a developed society all of these are important. This insight gave rise to the first of TLRP's ten principles, which, in common with the others, recognises the legitimacy of a normative dimension:

Principle 1: effective pedagogy equips learners for life in its broadest sense. Learning should aim to help individuals and groups to develop the intellectual, personal and social resources that will enable them to participate as active citizens, contribute to economic development and flourish as individuals in a diverse and changing society. This means adopting a broad conception of worthwhile learning outcomes and taking seriously issues of equity and social justice for all.

It is one thing to 'adopt a broad conception of worthwhile learning outcomes' for lifelong and life-wide learning; it is quite another to know whether ends are achieved. Dispositions and capabilities developed during the years of compulsory schooling can be enhanced or undermined by the opportunities and constraints experienced in later life.

In 2003 the Labour Government in England published its Every Child Matters agenda which highlighted the importance of five outcomes of the education system: being healthy; staying safe; enjoying and achieving; making a positive contribution; and achieving economic well-being. The UK Government also funded a Centre for Research on the Wider Benefits of Learning (WBL), which similarly viewed learning as a potential benefit to the individual, the family, the community and the nation. However, there is a tension between meeting these broad-ranging objectives, with which few disagree, and focusing on the basic skills and qualifications that have been the major thrust of contemporary policy. At the 2006 TLRP conference, where the ten principles were debated with researchers, a participant from the WBL Centre pointed out that although its longitudinal analysis of UK birth cohort studies provides much evidence of people's lives from birth to adulthood, 'these data sets do not have rich data on the experience of school. It would be useful to develop better integration between these approaches'. This must surely be a challenge for future researchers if we are to move from description of patterns in educational trajectories to better explanations of why they occur.

Curriculum, pedagogy and assessment (principles 2–5)

Conceptions of curriculum, pedagogy and assessment, and the interactions among them, lie at the heart of schooling. There has always been debate about what a whole curriculum should consist of, how it should be organised, what constitutes valued knowledge in a subject or field, how such knowledge can be represented and communicated to learners, and how learners' knowledge, understanding and skills can be detected and evaluated. These debates have involved curriculum developers, subject specialists, cognitive psychologists and assessment experts. However, in the 1970s, the intervention of a group of British sociologists (Young 1971), of which Basil Bernstein was the foremost, introduced a powerful new element into the debate.

They argued that knowledge, and hence curricula, are socially constructed and contested. This influenced a major shift in the way curricula were viewed. It appeared to undermine objectivity and led to some post-modernist claims that any knowledge, or form of curriculum organisation, is as valuable (or not) as any other, and the greatest need is to engage in rigorous critique of the political control they exercise. At its most extreme, this relativism seemed to undermine any Enlightenment notion that progress in education is possible because consensus on goals and means, undistorted by power relations, was thought to be unattainable.

TLRP's commitment to work 'to improve outcomes for learners' implied a belief that educational progress is possible. It never shared the extreme relativism of some post-modernists although it has tried to be inclusive of a wide range of theoretical perspectives within its activities. Pollard (2005, 3) viewed the Programme as a potential vehicle for 'creative mediation' and drew explicitly on an appeal to the Enlightenment commitment to the application of science and reason in the improvement of society. There is now wider evidence that researchers and scholars from a range of disciplines – epistemology, sociology, history, philosophy, cognitive science, curriculum theory, pedagogy and neuroscience – are 'bringing knowledge back' into play[12] to ask new kinds of questions and to ask some old questions in new ways. For example: Are pedagogies domain-specific? Do they need to vary between subjects and cultures? What is it to 'know' a subject and does this vary? How is knowledge constructed in different domains? What is the difference between a subject and a discipline, and is it ever possible for school pupils to develop an understanding of disciplines, given the fact that they study many subjects and are not immersed in a single discipline in the way that university students can be? Do students learn by acquiring knowledge or participating in practices? How can participation in communities of epistemic practice be validly and reliably assessed?

In this section, TLRP research and deliberation is brought to bear on these issues in justification of the following four principles that relate to the triad of curriculum, pedagogy and assessment.

Principle 2: effective pedagogy engages with valued forms of knowledge. Pedagogy should engage learners with the big ideas, key processes, modes of discourse, ways of thinking and practising, attitudes and relationships, which are the most valued learning processes and outcomes in particular contexts. They need to understand what constitutes quality, standards and expertise in different settings.

Principle 3: effective pedagogy recognises the importance of prior experience and learning. Pedagogy should take account of what the learner knows already in order for them, and those who support their learning, to plan their next steps. This includes building on prior learning but also taking account of the personal and cultural experiences of different groups of learners.

Principle 4: effective pedagogy requires learning to be scaffolded. Teachers, trainers and all those, including peers, who support the learning of others, should provide activities and structures of intellectual, social and emotional support to help learners to move forward in their learning. When these supports are removed the learning needs to be secure.

Principle 5: effective pedagogy needs assessment to be congruent with learning. Assessment should be designed and implemented with the goal of achieving maximum validity both in terms of learning outcomes and learning processes. It should help to advance learning as well as determine whether learning has occurred.

Learning presupposes that learners are learning something. This 'something' may be called 'knowledge' but what constitutes knowledge is often disputed. Gilbert Ryle's distinction between 'knowing that' and 'knowing how' has been important in expanding the conception beyond declarative knowledge to embrace procedural knowledge, although, in policy contexts, this is often reduced to a debate about learning facts versus learning skills.

In his keynote presentation, on the 'Complexity of Learning', to the 2005 TLRP Annual Conference, Michael Eraut delineated three types of knowledge: *codified knowledge,* judged by its source, truth claims and acceptability to 'gatekeepers'; *other cultural knowledge* as constructed and shared among communities and groups without undergoing codification; and *personal knowledge* defined as what people bring into new situations that enables them to think and act in those situations. This last type of knowledge comprises: codified knowledge ready for use; knowledge acquired during acculturation; knowledge constructed from experience, social inter-action and reflection; skills; and episodes, impressions and images (case knowl-edge). Eraut made the important point that: 'A person's performance nearly always uses several of these kinds of knowledge in some *integrated form*, and is influenced by both *context* and *feelings*' [his emphases]. Eraut was drawing particularly on his research into workplace professional learning[13] but these ideas are transferable to school learning. They support the argument implied in Principle 2, above, that a wide definition of what counts as valid knowledge, sensitive to context, should be valued.

A small number of TLRP schools projects focused very specifically on the learning of codified knowledge in subject domains. The project on The Role of Awareness in the Teaching and Learning of Literacy and Numeracy in Key Stage 2 (P4) focused upon aspects of learning to spell and learning fractions. This project was extended in Scotland but the Scottish project researched aspects of mathematics (proportion and ratio, referred to as 'intensive quantities') across school phases (P14). The Evidence-based Practice in Science Education (EPSE) network of projects (P7) worked mainly in secondary schools to investigate how learning in science can be enhanced. In all these projects, the difficulties in teaching concepts and processes could only be tackled successfully by engaging with cultural and personal knowledge, with context as a crucial variable.

Box 2

Evidence from school projects

The teaching of literacy in primary and infants schools is a 'hot topic' but little attention has been given to the potential value to junior age children of learning about the role of morphemes in spelling. The English language, with roots in many other languages, uses units of meaning called morphemes to form words.

The TLRP project on morphemes (P4) showed that literacy can be improved by increased awareness of how morphemes make words and are represented in spelling. It found that: (i) primary school children of all ages have difficulties with spelling words when the spelling cannot be predicted from the way the word sounds; (ii) children's difficulties with spelling of many words can be reduced by making them aware of the morphemes that compose words; and (iii) making children aware of morphemes has a positive effect on their vocabulary growth.

Fractions were the other focus of this project. It arose out of concern that rational numbers are not taught as well as natural numbers in primary school mathematics. A key finding was that knowledge of rational numbers is context-specific and needs to be developed in different situations where transfer is difficult. As with the morphemes work, the project developed a teaching programme that boosted pupils' understanding of the relative nature of fractions. The team found that: (i) most pupils in years 4 and 5 have not grasped the relative nature of fractions as numbers, and their difficulty is primarily conceptual; (ii) pupils have some intuitive understanding of the relative nature of fractions from their experiences with division; and (iii) teaching programmes that start from pupils' intuitions about sharing, and which establish connections to fractions as numbers, can have a positive impact on pupils' learning. The implications are that teaching needs to build on pupils' intuitions and be aware of the situations in which logical relations are most easily understood.

The project conducted in Scotland (P14) built on the observation that most mathematics teaching in the UK focuses on 'extensive quantities' involving one variable, such as distance or time, whilst 'intensive quantities', involving relationships between more than one variable, e.g. speed which involves distance in relation to time, tend to be ignored or treated in piecemeal fashion. The project found that: (i) primary school children of all ages have difficulties with intensive quantities, showing that mastery does not develop without teaching; (ii) these difficulties are primarily conceptual; but (iii) a mere two or three hours of teaching can boost children's understanding and their use of fractions.

The EPSE (evidence-based practice in science education) projects (P7) covered four distinct topics. One of these involved the design of short teaching sequences (4–6 lessons) to tackle important content that secondary pupils find difficult to learn: plant nutrition, modelling changes in matter in terms of particles, and the behaviour of simple electric circuits. When these teaching sequences were implemented, the researchers found that pupils' learning was measurably better, in terms of important aspects of conceptual understanding, than other pupils following the schools' normal approach to the same content, although they were no better than others at questions requiring factual recall. Testing regimes that focus heavily on factual recall may actually hide the need for such development because they can overestimate pupils' understanding of key ideas.

Another element of EPSE work focused on teaching pupils 'ideas about science' because much recent international debate has suggested that the primary aim of school science should be 'scientific literacy'. A Delphi study was used to explore the extent of agreement amongst a diverse group of expert stakeholders. The experts agreed on nine key epistemic themes: the nature of scientific knowledge (science and certainty; historical development of scientific knowledge), the methods of science (scientific methods and critical testing; analysis and interpretation of data; hypothesis and prediction; diversity of scientific thinking; creativity; science and questioning), and institutions and social practices in science (scientific work as communal and competitive activity). This led to an investigation of the nature of the challenge that teaching these ideas poses for teachers. The project concluded that these themes should be included in the school curriculum but this will require significant investment in the professional training of science teachers, particularly how to manage a more dialogic approach to teaching.

The findings of the ESPE projects fed directly into a TLRP Commentary on *Science education in schools* produced in collaboration with the Association for Science Education (T6) and also a suite of twenty-first century science GCSE courses, which has led to an increase in the number of youngsters choosing to study science at AS level.[14]

Another TLRP project focused on teaching and learning thinking skills through an 'infusion approach', i.e. linking patterns of thinking to specific curricular topics. Previous research and scholarship has demonstrated that thinking skills are not separate psychological abilities but learnable practices that are used for learning different subject matter. Again, the context is important.

The Thinking Skills project (P5) developed frameworks and classroom strategies with a curriculum topic and specific pattern of thinking being taught together. These methods were evaluated in a three-year study with Key Stage 2 pupils in Northern Ireland schools. A particular focus was on the development and analysis of classroom talk that helped children to think about their thinking (metacognition). The findings indicated that: (i) teachers were able to design and teach lessons using the infusion approach; (ii) children's thinking strategies were helped by such things as modelling thinking and using visual tools; (iii) 94 teachers involved in the CPD programme reported changes in their classroom practices, in their perceptions of children's thinking and in their images of themselves as teachers; and (iv) on self-rating measures, children reported positive changes in their learning, particularly their use of metacognitive strategies, which were related to effort. However these changes took time to build: those children who had participated for three years benefited most; and gains were not even across all learners. The 80% of children with moderate to high 'developed abilities', as measured by verbal and non-verbal reasoning tests, benefited most. When the bottom 20% were given problems to solve; they showed positive changes in their strategies compared to control children, but these specific achievements did not translate into how the children rated themselves more generally. Children's self-evaluations were positively correlated with measures of attainment in reading and mathematics but effects were small compared to the impact of background factors such as social-economic circumstances, gender, prior attainment and age in class. This shows just how powerful these background factors are. The study demonstrated that thinking skills and strategies are amenable to change but developing children's capacity to learn takes time and special attention needs to be paid to children with poorer cognitive and social resources.

The literacy, numeracy and thinking skills projects described in Box 2 were based in university departments of psychology. This raises an interesting question about whether forms of knowledge should be regarded primarily or exclusively as individual acquisitions of a cognitive nature. Does this take sufficient account of knowledge as embodied in social activity in communities of practice? Post-Vygotsky, educational researchers are aware of, and often sympathetic to, sociocultural claims that knowledge can only be constructed and revealed in and through social practices, especially through the use of shared language. Accordingly, consciousness, hence knowledge, is constantly being reinterpreted in dynamic interaction between mind and the world. The theoretical challenge faced by TLRP was deciding whether it could be a broad church, embracing a range of perspectives, from the cognitive to the sociocultural, even when these approaches appeared to contradict one another in rather fundamental ways.

The Learning Outcomes thematic group (T2), mentioned above, carried out an analysis of project documentation for evidence of Sfard's (1998) two metaphors of educational discourse: the acquisition metaphor (AM) and the participation metaphor (PM). This analysis showed that most TLRP projects stood on more than one 'metaphorical leg' (James and Brown 2005), confirming Sfard's perception that there are difficulties in choosing just one. Whilst theoretical coherence might be served by adopting a purist stance, the practical consequences can limit the goals and outcomes conceived as desirable in the variety of contexts for learning.

Anne Edwards, in her keynote presentation to the 2005 TLRP Annual Conference, pointed out that individual learning is underplayed in versions of sociocultural theory that are most interested in change in systems (e.g. Engeström 1999). However Engeström's transformative version of Activity Theory helps when working on new problems where innovative solutions are called for. In these circumstances neither acquisition nor strict participation approaches[15] to understanding learning help because there is need to go beyond what is already known in codified knowledge or cultural practice. From her Vygotskian stance, Edwards proposed 'relational agency' as a way of putting individual cognition back into the equation (Edwards 2005). She quoted Shotter (1993, 111): 'Vygotsky is concerned to study how people, through the use of their own social activities, by changing their own conditions of existence, can change themselves'.[16]

Most of the researchers involved in TLRP projects claimed to take a sociocultural, or social constructivist, theoretical position. Sometimes these two perspectives were clearly distinguished (e.g. P8); sometimes they were merged (e.g. P7).[17] The Programme, as a whole, had a commitment to interdisciplinary working, which implies a willingness to use the tools and constructs from diverse discourses. This has sometimes been difficult to achieve at project level, although:

> To capture the interacting layers of affordance and action, to acknowledge the power of history on practices and to reveal sense-making in language and tool use requires an educationally oriented team comprising sociologists, psychologists, socio-linguists, organisational experts and so on. (Edwards 2005, 13)

The group Edwards omitted to mention were neuroscientists. Yet increasingly, in the twenty-first century, interest has grown in brain research. In 2007, a TLRP thematic seminar series on neuroscience and education (T4) published a commentary (Howard-Jones 2007) to improve dialogue and collaboration between neuroscience and other educational, psychological and social science communities.[18] The significance of this publication lies in its 'cautious optimism'. Although brain imaging techniques, and other experiments, are giving fascinating results, the authors are sceptical of current 'brain-based applications' that have not, themselves, been properly evaluated. However, there is a belief that neuroscience does have relevance to education, which needs to be explored. As Howard-Jones (2007, 23) expressed it: '...collaborative research projects may need to extend the cognitive neuroscience model of brain>mind>behaviour to incorporate processes of social construction pertinent to learning'. If sociocultural views are seriously embraced then a model of behaviour>mind>brain would need to be considered, or, more appropriately, brain◇mind◇behaviour, which would capture the interactions between individual cognition and the material and social world. No TLRP projects investigated this directly but TLRP can claim that it established its importance for future research. The challenges however are considerable because this would require researchers, eminent in their own fields, to commit to working with others whose discourses and methods are unfamiliar.

The significance of domain knowledge (often referred to as content or subject knowledge) for effective pedagogy was also investigated by TLRP in another thematic seminar series (T8). In their position papers, developed to initiate and to summarise debate in two conferences, Moon and McCormick[19] formulated distinctions between knowledge, school knowledge and pedagogy. They based this on three clusters of ideas: the curriculum-orientated work of Shulman (1986), the cognitive approach of Gardner (1983, 1991) and the interrelated traditions of didactics and pedagogy in continental Europe (Verret 1975; Chevallard, 1991).

Shulman's distinction between subject content knowledge and pedagogical content knowledge has spawned a plethora of subject-specific research projects. However, Moon and McCormick criticise its objectivist epistemology, which implies that knowledge is a contained, fixed and external body of information. They also question his view of pedagogy as skills and knowledge that the teacher possesses, rather than as interaction in the process of learning.

In contrast, Gardner draws extensively on the transactional psychology of Dewey (and Bruner) to argue that while subjects or disciplines are important, it is necessary to move beyond them:

> ...organised subject matter represents the ripe fruitage of experiences... it does not represent perfection or infallible vision; but it is the best at command to further new experiences which may, in some respects at least, surpass the achievements embodied in existing knowledge or works of art. (Gardner 1992, 198)

According to Moon and McCormick this key insight still fails to address fully the issues thrown up by rapid and radical changes in domain knowledge. They therefore turn to Francophone literature, which explores the concept of 'didactic transposition' whereby subject knowledge is transformed into school knowledge. The work of Verret and, later, Chevallard emphasises that subject matter must undergo change, alteration and restructuring if it is to become teachable to novices or children. School knowledge becomes codified, partial and formalised in a syllabus, text or curriculum, which implies that learning has an initial state and an end state. This transformation of non-linear knowledge into programmable contents to be taught – termed didactics in the European tradition – is carefully distinguished from pedagogy, which is more about how to plan for, and respond to, problems and opportunities encountered in the flow of teaching and learning interactions.

Taking all these ideas together, Moon and McCormick present a model of the ways in which subject knowledge, school knowledge, pedagogic knowledge and personal constructs are related.[20] They illustrate this with an example from the perspective of a teacher of English (taken from Banks, Leach, and Moon 1999, 96, see Figure 2). Their discussion of codified knowledge, knowledge transformed through sociocultural processes, and personal knowledge, share much with Eraut's typology, outlined above.[21] Both accounts reflect an epistemological position that is neither purely objectivist nor entirely relativist. There is indeed 'stuff' to be learned

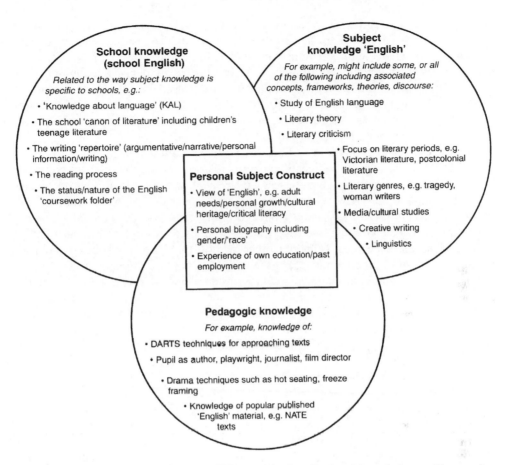

Figure 2. Banks, Leach, and Moon, 1999 model of professional knowledge as illustrated by teachers of English.

– ideas, facts, processes, stories, skills, language and dispositions – but it is equally important to learn that valued knowledge is produced, contested and changed in dialogic processes within and between communities of practice. This is the perspective that underpins TLRP's Principle 2 quoted above.

TLRP Principles 3 and 4, flow from the above discussion but focus more specifically on the ways in which knowledge is used in pedagogical processes to advance learning. These two principles are strongly linked and have theoretical and empirical foundations in the work of Dewey, Piaget, Vygotsky and Bruner.

The importance of taking account of prior learning, in cognitive terms, has been shown to be important in teaching and learning subjects such as mathematics and science where misconceptions established at an earlier stage create serious barriers to new learning and need to be tackled. TLRP projects in these subjects made this a particular focus. It was a feature of the EPSE project (P7), described in Box 2, which developed and evaluated sequences for teaching science concepts. It was also the focus of another EPSE project, which developed banks of diagnostic questions based on research about common misconceptions. The researchers found that carefully designed probes can provide quality information on pupils' understanding of key concepts, and inform action. However, they also found that the level of pupils' understanding of many fundamental science ideas is low, and increases only slowly with age. In other words, they cautioned that the level of challenge should not be underestimated. We should not be surprised by this conclusion. Support for the need to make associations with previous knowledge has largely been drawn from the psychological literature on meaning-making, but further evidence is emerging from neuroscience, which has linked this ability to activities in the inferior frontal lobes. The work of cognitive scientists, using fMRI scans, is beginning to show just how difficult it is to suppress naïve concepts of the physics taught in school curricula (see Dunbar, Fugelsang, and Stein 2007).

Mathematics and science are often described as cumulative subjects in which failure to understand basic concepts and principles leads to obvious difficulties in later learning. Other subjects have a less hierarchical or linear nature and the issues may seem less acute. However, the need to take account of prior learning still applies in different ways. What may be more important in these contexts – and is important in mathematics and science also – is to take account of understandings, skills and attitudes derived from the other worlds that pupils inhabit: from their homes, communities, media and peer groups. For example, a number of TLRP projects, especially those working with young children and/or investigating computer use, found benefits in teachers making more deliberate and positive use of the informal knowledge and understanding that children and young people acquire in their homes and local communities. This crucial aspect of effective pedagogy will be dealt with more fully in the section on personal and social processes and relationships, below. It has great significance for the equity dimensions of teaching and learning, as processes and in building identities. Another TLRP thematic seminar series (T10), on social diversity and difference, explored this further.

TLRP projects also had much to say about the 'scaffolding' of learning – an idea that was implicit in Vygotsky's work but named as such by Bruner (Wood, Bruner, and Ross 1976). Vygotsky's conception of learning as object-oriented, tool-mediated activity emphasises the importance of choice and use of tools, especially language tools, in learning activity. The role of the 'more expert other' in helping the novice to make progress in the zone of proximal development (ZPD) is equally crucial. When these two elements are brought together, the pertinence of the concept of scaffolding becomes evident. Within schools, it is often assumed that the responsibility for scaffolding lies primarily with the class teacher. However, TLRP projects in post-school settings remind us that often there is no 'teacher' in these contexts and effective scaffolding can be provided by peers or by computer programmes.[22] The key consideration, and the determinant of effectiveness, is whether tools – textbooks, computer programmes, other artefacts, signs, symbols and grading systems, etc. – are chosen and used appropriately. For example, tools such as interactive whiteboards are not intrinsically valuable; their worth depends on how they are used. As TLRP projects found, the usefulness of new technologies is associated with the ways in which they are incorporated into learning activity and classroom dialogue.

Box 3

Evidence from school projects

The INTERPLAY project (P1) investigated how practitioners can create opportunities for learning with ICTs in play settings involving very young children. Prac-

---

titioners and researchers worked together using the concept of 'guided interaction'. They found that: (i) children's encounters with ICTs are enhanced when practitioners use guided interaction (questioning, modelling, praising, supporting) and balanced child-initiated and adult-led activities; (ii) encounters with ICT accompanied by guided interaction can enhance dispositions to learn, knowledge of the world and operational skills, as well as hand–eye coordination; and (iii) providing a broad range of ICTs, including digital still and video cameras, mobile phones and electronic keyboards and toys, as well as computers, promotes more opportunities for learning.

The InterActive Education project (P8) worked in partnership with primary and secondary school teachers to investigate ways in which ICT can be used to enhance learning in subject domains, particularly its value in helping children to enter new knowledge worlds. The approach was explicitly sociocultural. The project found that: (i) effective teaching and learning with ICT involves building bridges between 'idiosyncratic' learning, arising from extended periods of individual engagement, and 'intended' learning that often needs to be supported by the teacher, e.g. pupils are unlikely to develop knowledge of science from game-like simulation software without help; (ii) there is a two-way exchange of knowledge between home and school use of ICT and this impacts on school learning; and (iii) the teacher can promote successful use of ICT by helping pupils build on out-of-school learning to construct 'common' knowledge which has currency in communities beyond the classroom.

A linked project on the use of ICT to improve learning and attainment through interactive teaching (P16) focused particularly on the use of interactive whiteboards. The proliferation of interactive whiteboard (IWB) technology in classrooms suggests that teachers and educational policy makers see this as a very powerful teaching tool. The project found that although IWBs have the potential to support new forms of interactivity in teaching, and more participatory pedagogy, they are still tools that need to be used well, which has implications for teachers' professional learning, especially the development of their pedagogical reasoning.

Robin Bevan, a TLRP research training fellow, carried out a PhD project[23] in which he investigated on-screen learning in secondary schools using a concept-mapping software program developed in the United States. Bevan's study showed how effectiveness of on-screen activity depends significantly on the strategy adopted by the teacher. He found that: (i) pupils who used the on-screen concept-mapping tool alone, with no collaboration with other students, achieved no significant sustained learning gains; (ii) when the class collaborated in developing their concept maps, pupils demonstrated sustained and improved learning in a subsequent essay task; but (iii) providing automated scoring for the concept maps demotivated the weakest pupils and did not lead to any additional learning gains. He concluded that despite the promise of new technologies, an unmediated switch to on-screen learning is unlikely to lead to improvements in learning. Teachers looking for improved learning with on-screen activities need to explore the powerful potential of peer collaboration. Indeed the adoption of new classroom strategies involving such collaboration can be more significant than the impact of the software itself.

The conclusions from the examples given in Box 3 are corroborated by other TLRP projects. The numeracy and literacy projects (P4 and P14) were centrally concerned with creating explicit scaffolds for teachers to use. And the thinking framework developed by the Thinking Skills project (P5) was itself a scaffold. Like the Inter-Play project (P1), the very large-scale EPPE 3-11 Project (P2) also provided evidence of the importance of both adult-initiated and child-initiated activity, including direct teaching and sustained shared thinking.

What emerges from all this evidence is the primacy of dialogue. But dialogue needs to be understood, not simply as oral interactions in classrooms, but as more varied communications between minds. Alexander (2006, 13) gives credit to Bakhtin (1981) for providing a vocabulary for exploring the nature and possibilities of dialogue. Bakhtin was interested in the relationship between the individual and society, present and past, between the developing mind and the thinking embodied in the wider culture, between our inner and outer worlds. While face-to-face interactions are important, a dialogue can be set up between authors and their readers so that readers have access to the author's thinking and can use it to interrogate their own. The breadth of these ideas is reflected in 'enacting dialogue', one of twelve aims for primary education distilled from the Cambridge Primary Review, which describes advancing pedagogy through dialogue 'between self and others, between personal and collective knowledge, between past and present, between different ways of making sense' (Alexander 2010, 199).

The dialogic approach that Alexander has been developing through his international research (Alexander 2001, 2006) comprises a three-part repertoire informed by five dialogic principles. The repertoire consists of *learning talk* (narrating, explaining, questioning, answering, analysing, speculating, imagining, exploring, evaluating, discussing, arguing, justifying and negotiating), *teaching talk* (rote, recitation, exposition, discussion, dialogue) and *interactive strategies* (whole-class teaching, teacher-led group work, pupil-led group work, one-to-one pupil discussion, one-to-one discussion between pupil and teacher). The principles that inform this repertoire are that genuine dialogue is *collective, reciprocal, supportive, cumulative and purposeful*. According to Alexander, the most vital of these is cumulation: that teachers and pupils build on their own and each other's ideas and chain them into coherent lines of thinking and enquiry. 'If an answer does not give rise to a new question from itself, it falls out of the dialogue' (Bakhtin 1986, 168). However, this principle is also the most difficult to achieve, which has major implications for 'assessment for learning' (AfL), the pedagogical strategy that has been promoted extensively, by researchers and policy makers, in the UK and internationally.

Box 4

Evidence from school projects

The TLRP Learning How to Learn project (LHTL) (P13) built on existing research which demonstrated that assessment for learning (formative assessment) practices can lead to improved learning and achievement (Black and Wiliam 1998; Black et al. 2003). Four clusters of practices have been identified, all of which are based on dialogue: developing classroom talk and questioning to elicit understanding; giving appropriate feedback; sharing criteria of quality; and peer-

and self-assessment which incorporate elements of all three previous clusters of practices. The strand of the LHTL project that focused on classrooms showed that assessment for learning helps teachers promote learning how to learn activity, which enables pupils to become more autonomous learners. Thereby, classroom practice becomes better aligned with the educational values expressed by teachers, and less driven by a culture of performativity. However, analysis of video evidence from classrooms showed how difficult it is to shift from reliance on specific techniques, 'dropped into' conventional lessons, e.g. writing learning objectives on the board (the 'letter' of AfL). Such techniques swiftly become mechanistic, ritualised and distorted in their purposes. For example, the use of 'traffic lights' as a means for pupils to indicate their confidence in their learning as a lesson progresses, easily becomes just another way of scoring products (James et al. 2006, 99–100). What is needed is a more holistic transformation based on deeper principles – such as thinking about the questions posed by an answer to a previous question – integrated into the flow of pedagogical interactions (the 'spirit' of AfL). Marshall and Drummond (2006), drawing on Dewey's conception of progressive education, described this as requiring 'high organisation based upon ideas'. The LHTL project demonstrated that, although advice on specific techniques is useful in the short term, longer-term development and sustainability depends on re-evaluating beliefs about learning, reviewing the way learning activities are structured, and rethinking classroom roles and relationships.

The aims of the Learning How to Learn project (P13) – to develop, embed and spread assessment for learning practice in ways that promote autonomous learning by pupils– was in line with TLRP's Principle 5 that, 'Effective pedagogy needs assessment to be congruent with learning', and especially that, 'It should help to advance learning as well as determine whether learning has occurred'. This project focused very specifically on the relationship between assessment and learning and how a beneficial synergy might be established.

A related element of Principle 5: 'Assessment should be designed and implemented with the goal of achieving maximum validity both in terms of learning outcomes and learning processes' was specifically addressed by other projects, and by two thematic initiatives (T9, T13). Traditionally, the quality of assessments is judged by their reliability and their validity, which together indicate whether the inferences drawn from assessment results are dependable. Often more attention is paid to reliability for two reasons. First, there are clear technical procedures for enhancing reliability; second, the publication of unreliable results can have immediate and far-reaching political and personal consequences.[24] However, there is a sense in which even reliable assessment results have no worth if they are not valid – if they have no meaning. Kane (2001) traces the development of validity theory over a century, from limited criterion-related models, through sophisticated construct models, to an argument-based approach. The current view is that validation requires an extended analysis of evidence, based on explicit statements of proposed interpretations, and consideration of competing interpretations.

Validity is concerned with the clarification and justification of the intended interpretations and uses of observed scores (sic). It is notoriously difficult to pin down the interpretation (meaning) of an observation (hence the popularity of detective novels). (Kane 2001, 339)

What Kane makes clear is that validity cannot be achieved by the manipulation of statistical models; it requires qualitative analysis and judgement and is therefore open to contestation. In high stakes environments this is not easy to accept and the most powerful people in a system are inclined to limit potential damage by limiting the scope for dispute. In so doing they often also limit the validity of assessments.

Box 5

Evidence from school projects

The problem of limited validity in standard assessments was illustrated in the EPSE projects (P7), which showed that, although learning about the nature of science is valued, current assessment regimes privilege recall of science 'facts' over epistemic understanding. Furthermore, emphasis on factual recall (as in KS3 science tests before 2008) overestimates conceptual understanding because a single short-answer question is often taken as evidence of understanding of a more complex construct. In these circumstances more than one question is usually needed to ensure that the inferences drawn from the results are valid.

The need to avoid overestimating or underestimating children's capabilities was also raised as an issue by the INTERPLAY project (P1), which explored the possibilities of recording what children were actually doing with ICTs by using these tools for capturing evidence. This has the virtue of authenticity and the benefit of monitoring progress in real time. However, it depends on teachers and other adults accepting a role for which they may feel ill-equipped without additional training.

As the LHTL project discovered (P13), the constraints of an accountability system, which encourages teaching to the test through the publication of league tables, does little to promote the openness and honestly needed for a system based principally on on-going teacher assessments. Yet openness would be the prime condition needed to fulfil the requirements for validity that Kane outlines.

Two other groups of TLRP projects, not mentioned before but referred to more fully in the next section, noted other limitations of existing assessment measures. The Understanding and Developing Inclusive Practices in Schools network of projects (P11) and the linked Facilitating Teacher Engagement in more Inclusive Practice project (P9) highlighted the need for assessments of a broader range of outcomes than those evaluated in conventional tests and examinations, including pupil participation and development of learner identities.

The Group Work projects (P6, P12) used a multiplicity of measures in their research to evaluate pupil development in cognitive, social and affective domains. These covered a wide range of processes and outcomes relevant to all kinds of outcomes. However, they noted that group work itself tends not to be directly assessed, in summative terms, despite the value attached by employers to both group products and teamwork skills. This is not to say that it cannot be done. Galton (2010) reviews possible ways of assessing both group productivity and individual contributions and argues that fair, reliable and valid assessment of both these elements is possible. However, it is undoubtedly difficult, and it demands that teachers and pupils understand the criteria for judgement.

The essence of the general problem, illustrated in Box 5, was identified by the Learning Outcomes thematic group:

> If projects within TLRP are attempting to conceptualise learning outcomes in a much broader way than previously, taking account of surface and deep, process and product, individual and social, intended and emergent learning, how can these 'outcomes' be detected in a way that does them justice? (James and Brown 2005, 18)

No TLRP schools projects were established with a prime intention to develop new assessment instruments. Many had assumed that they would be able to use existing measures to detect the outcomes in which they were interested. National tests and examinations (e.g. GCSE) were widely used as proxy measures of attainment, together with cognitive abilities tests (e.g. PIPS in P3, P6, P12), and self-report inventories of metacognition, motivation or attitudes towards learning (e.g. ELLI in P3; ALCPs in P5).[25] However, the choice was motivated as much by the need to have some measure of change over time, across cases or in comparison with control groups, as by the need for construct validity. The desire to reconceptualise learning outcomes and the need to investigate change were fundamentally in tension. On the one hand, investigating change usually requires some baseline assessment, which encourages the use of existing measures; on the other hand, new conceptions of learning outcomes require new measures and these demand extensive development and trialling. This situation, created mainly by the conditions of TLRP commissioning, was unsatisfactory. Little could be done to change the situation for currently funded projects but a thematic group was set up to explore the issues further.

The Assessment of Significant Learning Outcomes (ASLO) thematic group (T9), which drew on the expertise of the UK Assessment Reform Group,[26] set out to examine the relationships between assessment and pedagogy and between assessment and curriculum, and, specifically, issues of alignment or congruence. Five case studies were chosen to investigate how the assessment of learning outcomes was understood in different contexts: school mathematics in England; Learning to Learn in countries of the European Union; workplace learning in the UK; higher education in UK; and vocational education in England. Three initial questions were used to frame the enquiry:

(1) What are the significant learning outcomes that are not being assessed in a system that relies wholly on test-based assessment procedures?
(2) What are the indicators of student performance, which have been, or could be, developed in relation to such learning outcomes?
(3) What assessment procedures do not rely on testing but do, or might, give dependable measures of student performance?

'Curriculum' and 'assessment' were seen in fundamentally different ways in each context, and, in only two of the five settings, was the term 'learning outcomes' in widespread use. However, four common themes emerged across the five case studies: construct definition; progression; the impact of assessment procedures; system-level accountability as a driver of alignment. The familiar problem of construct definition – how, and by whom, the constructs involved are defined and made real – was exemplified by school mathematics.

Current views about what school mathematics should be are often quite different. One view is that mathematics is the performance of routine algorithms; another sees mathematics as a tool to tackle 'everyday' or 'real world' problems. The former leads to assessment of achievement with well-defined exercises, which have a single right answer, with learners inclined to think of achievement as arriving at that answer. The latter looks for evidence of a capacity to tackle the rather messy contexts which are characteristic of everyday problems: problems for which there is no right answer, and where explanation of the way the problem has been defined, and of the approach adopted, is as important as the 'answer' itself. Such work is much more demanding to guide, and harder to assess. [...]

The testing system is of course of crucial importance here. With time-limited tests to cover a very full curriculum, any activity that involves much more time, than that in which a single examination answer can be given, is not possible. Therefore, realistic problems are ruled out. This results in an invalidity block, which could in principle be cleared by strengthening the use of teachers' own assessments in national tests and public examinations. (Mansell, James and the Assessment Reform Group 2009, 14)

The conclusion from this aspect of the ASLO enquiry was that the constructs underpinning programmes of study are often inadequately articulated.

Enabling progression is at the heart of pedagogy and therefore central to formative assessment (assessment for learning), however, the ASLO case studies showed that summative assessment requirements, driven by pressure for uniformity and accountability, often constrain teachers from using their own judgement to nurture progression. Equally, the impact of assessment procedures on the alignment between intended and actual learning outcomes is considerable. Misalignment in this respect can represent a threat to the integrity of learning itself. The examples studied highlighted numerous ways in which assessment procedures disrupted desirable learning or encouraged undesirable learning. Case studies – such as the project to develop a European indicator for learning to learn capability[27] – also revealed just how influential the political imperatives for system-level accountability can be. 'They drive the role of assessment in defining the relevant constructs and, perhaps more crucially, shape how teachers and students then interpret and enact those constructs.' (Daugherty 2009, 3).

The evidence of the ASLO thematic work suggests that the relationship between assessment and curriculum is more multi-dimensional and multi-level than the terms 'alignment' or 'congruence' imply. The group concluded that it might be better understood as a complex, non-linear, interacting system with the ultimate goal being a synergy of curriculum, pedagogy and assessment. This takes us back to the proposition at the very beginning of this section.

Ideas and evidence from the ASLO seminar were incorporated into a TLRP Commentary on *Assessment in Schools. Fit for Purpose*? (T13). This was also prepared with the help of the Assessment Reform Group (ARG) (Mansell, James and the Assessment Reform Group 2009). Its purpose was to present policy makers – in the run-up to the 2010 general election – with four key challenges drawn from the collective research intelligence of TLRP and ARG. In light of the evidence that assessment systems in the UK, and elsewhere, are expected to serve an enormous range of purposes – many of them quite remote from their original intentions to evaluate what a pupil knows, understands and can do – education professionals, policy makers and the public should be aware of the unintended consequences of assessment policy decisions and initiatives. At the heart of the matter are concerns about fitness for purpose, which are also about the quality of assessments. The commentary identified different criteria for judging such quality depending on whether the purpose was formative, summative or evaluative. It contested the common view that a single set of assessments could serve several purposes without distorting one purpose or another. The four challenges were therefore: to extend, embed and spread good in-class assessment practice through the professional development of teachers; to enhance confidence in tests and examinations by improving their reliability and validity; to justify the costs of the assessment system, which in England was calculated as £750 million per annum; and to avoid micro-management by politicians and managers who are ill-equipped to make technical judgements of quality. Above all, assessment systems must be congruent with the overarching purpose of education systems to advance learning.

One of the outputs (Filer and Pollard 2000), from the TLRP Associate projects on Identity and Learning (P21), shed light on assessment from a different angle by focusing specifically on pupil perspectives, strategies, relationships and identities developed in assessment encounters. As in other contexts of schooling, children develop their identities through successive experiences as they move through schooling. Experiences of assessment are shown to be among the most powerful. As in the TLRP project on Consulting Pupils on the Assessment of their Learning (P15), which also focused on pupil perspectives, assessment is revealed as a social process. Performance is inseparable from context and results take meaning from social and cultural interpretation. The case for strengthening the validity of the inferences drawn from assessments is therefore overwhelming if learners' sense of agency and identity is to be promoted and not destroyed.

Personal and social processes and relationships (principles 6–8)

This cluster of principles also reflects contemporary awareness of the influence of social, as well as psychological, factors on learning. As noted above, TLRP funded psychologists such as Peter Bryant and Terezinha Nunes (P4) and Christine Howe (P14), and neuroscientists such as Paul Howard-Jones (T4), although the major disciplinary framework from which it drew was that of education itself. In this respect, the Programme reflected the contemporary UK field with an eclectic mix of projects, many informed by sociological and sociocultural theory. For example, several projects shared an interest in Bourdieu and another group identified with activity theory. Some, particularly those concerned with identity, were influenced by the symbolic interactionist roots of British qualitative sociology of education.

Most TLRP projects started from specific educational issues but explicitly maintained a theoretically-informed awareness of agency, culture and context in education. The outcomes of such work are reflected in the three principles below.

Principle 6: effective pedagogy promotes the active engagement of the learner. A chief goal of teaching and learning should be the promotion of learners' independence and autonomy. This involves acquiring a repertoire of learning strategies and practices, developing positive learning dispositions, and having the will and confidence to become agents in their own learning.

Principle 7: effective pedagogy fosters both individual and social processes and outcomes. Learners should be encouraged and helped to build relationships and communication with others for learning purposes, in order to assist the mutual construction of knowledge and enhance the achievements of individuals and groups. Consulting learners about their learning and giving them a voice is both an expectation and a right.

Principle 8: effective pedagogy recognises the significance of informal learning. Informal learning, such as learning out of school or away from the workplace, should be recognised as at least as significant as formal learning and should therefore be valued and appropriately utilised in formal processes.

In relation to Principle 6, almost all TLRP schools projects affirmed the importance of developing active engagement, positive learning dispositions, self-confidence and learning awareness. Indeed, in an era that saw a steady growth, within much of the UK, of central control over curriculum, pedagogy and assessment, the engagement of learners has become an increasingly pressing contemporary issue.

Traditionally, in psychological terms, such issues have been framed in terms of motivation with emphasis being placed on ways of engaging individual learners in particular tasks. The work of Carol Dweck (1999) for instance, on 'mastery' and 'learned helplessness' as orientations to new learning challenges, has been very influential in the UK. In parallel, though, has been a practical humanistic tradition in British education drawing on the practitioner enquiry movement initiated by Lawrence Stenhouse (1975). TLRP's network on Consulting Pupils about Teaching and Learning (P10) was a manifestation of this commitment to practical theorising and improvement. Led by the late Jean Ruddock, the Consulting Pupils network directly engaged teachers, children and young people in 46 schools in reflection on their classroom practices and school experiences (Rudduck and McIntyre 2007). Indirectly, it connected with thousands more in building from the UN Convention on the Rights of the Child (1989) in affirming the quality and constructive nature of feedback about teaching and learning that pupils were able to offer. Outcomes (see evidence Box 6 below) included enhanced commitment to learning and improved teacher–pupil relationships. The work was widely influential and contributed, for example, to provision for pupil opinions in the framework through which all schools in England were externally inspected.

The UK tradition of qualitative sociology has also developed to offer a complementary understanding of how learners perceive and make sense of their school experiences. For example, the Identity and Learning Programme, a TLRP associate investment (P21), was a longitudinal series of ethnographic projects by Pollard and Filer tracking two cohorts of children from age 4 to 16 (e.g. Pollard and Filer 1999). It started in the mid 1980s and demonstrated how pupils progressively develop strategies to cope with the challenges of schooling over time, and how secure forms of learning become embedded in meaningful personal narratives and identities. Where school curricula fail to make meaningful connections with the learner, then it is argued that pupil performance and capability are likely to be shallow and transitory. Similar ideas were reflected in other TLRP projects. A developed example is provided by a study of further education experiences – Transforming Learning Cultures (James and Biesta 2007) – which recognised the way in which institutional conditions enable or constrain opportunities for independent learning. Another is that of Crozier and colleagues (2009) who analysed disjunctions in the experiences of working class students entering higher education.

However, the analysis was developed most thoroughly by the Learning Lives project (Biesta et al. 2011) which studied learners across the lifecourse using a combination of evidence from a large-scale cohort study and case study interviews reviewing learning careers over time.[28] This study was important for its lifelong reach and demonstration of the durability of attitudes deriving from early school experiences. In particular, it reported how narratives about learning and educational experiences are used as frameworks of interpretation in the development of identity, self-confidence and agency.

A seminar series on Transitions through the Lifecourse was established to explore such ideas across TLRP projects (T17). Through this work, transitions between sectors at different phases of life were reviewed – home to school, school to college, college and university, between workplaces – and analyses of social class, gender, disability and age patterns were also undertaken (Ecclestone, Biesta, and Hughes 2010). The emerging analysis was initially seen as a possible way of constructing a meta-narrative for the TLRP programme as a whole, since the work of many projects could be plotted across dimensions of the lifecourse. As it developed, the interest in transitions deepened because of the discontinuities and disruption to progression in learning that was often observed. The social dimension remained prominent in the thinking of TLRP teams. As John Field suggested in his introduction to an edited collection on this work, it is necessary to recognise the 'diversity of individual experience' but we 'should not neglect the collective dimensions to transition'. He went on: 'we need to examine systematically the sites in which learning occurs and the nature of locally experienced structures of opportunity' (Field 2010, xxiii).

Here then we can clearly see the emphasis on the social of a significant cluster of TLRP projects, and their concern for the construction of meaning in relation to circumstances. The promotion of learner independence and autonomy, in this sense, is not just about the effectiveness of learning. It also concerns the realisation of rights, formation as a person, manifestation of citizenship and contribution of individuals to history.

Box 6

Evidence from school projects

Consulting Pupils about Teaching and Learning (P10), a network of six projects, built on growing recognition that young people have a right to be heard and have something worthwhile to say about their school experiences. However, listening to and learning from pupils is a challenge to teachers and schools. The findings of the projects, drawn primarily from the testimony of pupils and teachers, provided evidence of benefits for: (i) pupils, by enhancing engagement with learning, sense of agency and of self as learner; (ii) teachers, by deepening insights into children's abilities and learning preferences, leading to more responsive teaching and willingness to give pupils more responsibility; (iii) schools, by strengthening school policy in substantive rather than marginal or tokenistic ways; and (iv) national policy, by providing new insights and practical tools for school self-evaluation and development planning. Importantly, however, given the increasing status of 'pupil voice' as a 'movement', this research also cautioned that ingrained habits often prevent pupils being heard. Conditions for new ways of listening include: hearing the quiet voice in the acoustic of the school; avoiding the creation of a pupil voice elite; maintaining authenticity; sharing data and/or offering feedback to pupils; trust and openness as a pre-condition of dialogue and action.

This project was extended by subsequent work carried in Northern Ireland with a particular focus on children's rights to be consulted on the assessment of their learning. This had particular relevance in Northern Ireland as policy makers introduced a Pupil Profile to record pupils' development and encourage the adoption of Assessment for Learning in classroom practice. The CPAL project (P15) comprised three independent but interrelated studies in primary and post-primary schools. One of these asked (through focus groups, creative approaches and e-consultation) 80 Key Stage 2 pupils what they thought of the concept of the Pupil Profile, and another study investigated teachers' and parents' awareness of children's rights and their responses to key aspects of AfL pedagogy. Findings were that: (i) KS2 pupils viewed Pupil Profiles as personal documents, useful for helping them improve their learning and helping them with decision-making about future schooling; (ii) to fulfil these expectations, children thought that Profiles should provide feedback from teachers on how to improve, be attractive and readable, include a section contributed by pupils, have input from parents/carers, be inclusive of wider abilities and achievements, and enhance a pupils' views of themselves; and (iii) teachers advocated children's rights, expressed by Article 12 of UNCRC and embodied in AfL practices, but viewed time, class size, curriculum coverage, need for control and school culture as constraining implementation. CPAL demonstrates that pupils can be consulted directly on significant matters of educational policy, and that where principles of AfL are embedded in practice, pupils can experience high levels of participation.

Pollard and Filer's longitudinal ethnography, Identity and Learning (P21), focused on the interaction between pupils' experiences of schools, homes and communities in the formation of learner identities. Two cohorts of children (ten in each of two primary schools contrasted by different social class settings) were tracked through multiple secondary schools to public examinations at age 16. Analysis of detailed case studies from this project revealed that: (i) relationships between teachers and pupils remain the basis of the moral order of the classroom and underpin discipline and behaviour; (ii) children develop their identities as learners through successive experiences as they move through schooling; (iii) pupils actively negotiate their way through schooling, which, over time, can be conceptualised as a 'pupil career'; and (iv) the extent to which school provision matches learners' identities, social relationships and cultural resources strongly influences the outcomes of education.

Principle 7 focuses on how teaching and learning foster both individual and social processes and outcomes. Practitioners consistently assert the importance of 'good relationships' in classrooms or, to put it another way, the necessity for teacher–pupil respect as the foundation of discipline, order and learning. Indeed, the longitudinal work of TLRP's associated Identity and Learning project (P21) claimed that 'meaning and opportunity in classrooms build from everyday relationships' (Pollard and Filer 2007) – thus encapsulating the interrelationship of individual perspectives and social interaction. Some projects used the concept of social capital (Putnam 1993) in discussion of broad social opportunities whilst noting the formative role that school and classroom processes and peer-relations can play in such accumulation.

More specifically, several TLRP projects investigated the particular educational uses to which such relationships and processes can be put. For example, reference has been made earlier to the projects on thinking skills, learning how to learn and pupil consultation.

The TLRP Group Work projects (P12 and P6) particularly demonstrate the benefits of efforts to improve student's mastery of cooperation and collaboration. Pupils involved in such developments made significant academic gains, which were stable across schools in different social contexts. The implications are that group work can produce significant benefits to attainment, motivation and behaviour. However, this requires explicit preparation and support. Group work skills need to be approached developmentally: social skills first, then communication skills, then problem-solving. Providing teachers with practical 'relational' strategies, based on principles, provides a successful approach to raising standards and improving behaviour – and thus moves beyond the general affirmation of relationships. A TLRP Research Training Fellowship study (Bevan, Pedder, and Carmichael 2007) of on-screen learning using concept-mapping software also found that significant sustained learning gains were only associated with structured opportunities for collaborative peer discussion. These projects confirm the vital importance of classroom dialogue when it is put to use in building explicit awareness of learning processes.

Box 7

Evidence from school projects

The SPRinG (Social Pedagogic Research into Group work) project (P12) sought to develop a new approach to increasing engagement and learning in everyday classroom settings at Key Stage 1 (led by Kutnick), Key Stage 2 (led by Blatchford) and Key Stage 3 (led by Galton). The project team was aware of a wide gap between the potential of group work to enhance learning and previous evidence of its limited use in schools. The problems that they identified were a lack of a strategic view of the purpose of groups and practical problems of formation and process. In response, the team embarked on a project to work with teachers to develop a programme of group work that could be successfully integrated into school life (the development stage) followed by a year-long intervention study to evaluate the success of the programme in terms of attainment, motivation and within-group interactions, compared to control groups (the evaluation stage). An applications stage was designed to apply group work to contexts known to be particularly problematic. The project found that: (i) in contrast to views that group work may interfere with learning in mainstream curricular areas, teachers successfully implemented effective group work in both primary and secondary school classrooms and across the curriculum; (ii) this had a positive effect on pupil's academic progress and higher conceptual learning (at KS1 effect sizes from 0.22 to 0.62 were recorded in reading and mathematics; at KS2, where science was a special focus of the project; effect sizes from 0.21 to 0.58 were recorded for conceptual understanding and inferential thinking); (iii) there were positive effects on pupil behaviour, through increased on-task interactions, more equal participation, sustained interactions and higher level discussions; and (iv) there were improvements in personal relations between teachers and pupils and among pupils, provided that teachers took the time to train pupils in the skills of group working.

A linked project in Scotland (ScotSPRinG) (P6) had similar results. This project worked in primary schools and investigated the effects of class composition in urban and rural school contexts where classes may be single age or a mix of year groups. As with the Key Stage 2 study in England, the team worked with upper primary school age pupils and focused upon the development of conceptual understanding in science, although a range of cognitive, affective and social measures were used to assess impact of innovations. Project findings showed: (i) significant gains across a number of measures, attributable to the group work intervention; (ii) cognitive gains were related to the quality of collaborative dialogue during group work; (iii) there were no consistent differences between single age or mixed age classes, nor between urban and rural schools; and (iv) group work yielded significant gains in social relations with collaborative engagement with tasks contributing most, however, socio-emotional gains were independent of the cognitive gains. The practical 'relational' strategies offered to teachers were highly valued and reported to benefit both teachers' professional practice and pupils' learning, which implies that the SPRinG approach is effective and sustainable.

Principle 8 asserts the significance of informal learning and urges its utilisation in more formal educational settings. This principle can thus be expressed simply, but has profound implications and challenges. Recognition of the social and cultural dimensions of learning in many TLRP projects produced a heightened awareness of learners, relationships and contexts. In successive annual Programme conferences, researchers struggled with how to study, analyse and represent the learning that took place beyond formal educational settings. Two seminar series were established to wrestle with these issues.

The first seminar series was entitled, Contexts, Communities and Networks: Mobilising Learners' Resources and Relationships in Different Domains (T16, see Edwards, Biesta, and Thorpe 2009). Meeting over a two-year period, representatives of projects and others explored the nature of learning in different settings and the validity, or otherwise, of contrastive descriptions of these processes. Sociocultural theory provided a major driver here. So, for example, a study of literacy practices in further education (Ivanic et al. 2009) demonstrated how learners' everyday, vernacular experience yielded significant educational value when ways were found to draw on this knowledge in college settings. This approach echoed Dewey's emphasis on the validity of many different kinds of experience. The implications for pedagogy are profound. As Thorpe and Mayes (2009, 160) put it in their review of the work of the seminar series:

> Pedagogy needs to build connections across different areas of experience, between the classroom, the workplace, the home and social life, where these connections can provide points of engagement for learners and ways of enabling them to draw on the resources of their own experience.

A second TLRP investment was led by Leon Feinstein and drew, beyond the Programme, on the work of the Centre for the Wider Benefits of Learning (WBL) at the University of London, Institute of Education (T15, see Schuller et al. 2004; Feinstein, Budge et al. 2008). This Centre specialises in analysis of social, economic, medical and environmental factors influencing learning across the lifecourse and draws on both qualitative research and large-scale statistical analysis of cohort, economic and social data. TLRP's portfolio of projects, though rather different in nature, echoed the Centre's range of concerns and an association was therefore developed. In particular, whilst WBL worked on patterns in life trajectories, TLRP focused on pedagogic and learning processes. This work came together in a Foresight publication for the UK Government Office for Science entitled *Learning through life: Future challenges* (Feinstein, Vorhaus, and Sabates 2008). Citing TLRP's Ten Principles, this report argued that only quality education and learning can enhance skill and capability.

In England, the New Labour government did indeed demonstrate greater awareness of the significance of social context in relation to children and young people. For example, as noted earlier, the Every Child Matters agenda and integration of national health, social and educational provision into Children's Services across the whole country were clear evidence of holistic analysis and of attempts to promote inclusion through the coordination of services.

TLRP's own work in these areas was at rather different levels, whether in workplace, university or school education. Two areas of research stand out regarding school education – home–school relations and the influence of new technologies.

The Home-School Knowledge Exchange (HSKE) project (P3, see Hughes 2006), investigated how the home and school environments for learning might complement each other. Focusing upon literacy and numeracy in these two worlds, the team helped teachers, parents and children to find new ways of exchanging knowledge between home and primary school, using videos, photographs, shoeboxes of artefacts, etc. They then investigated how this process of knowledge exchange could enhance learning and ease the transition to secondary school.

Explicit home–school knowledge exchange activities produced impact on outcomes but this was mediated by social class, gender and attainment – factors that underline the importance of handling informal learning with sensitivity in order to avoid negative consequences for particular groups of pupils.

Box 8

Evidence from school projects

The Home-School Knowledge Exchange project (P3) collected baseline data in 'action' and 'comparison' schools in Bristol and Cardiff prior to instigating a range of home–school exchange activities. Measures were repeated and qualitative pupil/family case studies were also developed to assist in the interpretation of the patterns found. The project concluded that: (i) there are substantial 'funds of knowledge', embedded in national, ethnic and popular cultures of homes and communities, which can be used to support learning in schools; (ii) simple knowledge-exchange activities can make teachers more knowledgeable about children's out-of-school lives, and parents more knowledgeable about what happens in school; and (iii) home–school knowledge exchange can have a positive impact on teachers, parents and children and on attainment although gains were not statistically significant in mathematics, and not uniform across the project in literacy (they were significantly better in Cardiff schools than in Bristol).

A research training fellowship, held by Brookes,[29] was linked to the HSKE project and focused particularly on provision for gifted and talented pupils at secondary transfer. Findings from this ethnographic study tracking 15 Year 5 children into Year 8 show how school selection by parents, and the process of transfer, are experienced as multi-faceted, iterative, stressful and prolonged.[30]

Another of TLRP's associated projects is of relevance here. EPPE (Effectiveness of Pre-school Primary Education) (P2) is the most significant European study to date on the impact of pre-school and the contribution of family background to children's development (3–11 years old) (see Sylva et al. 2010). The findings from the pre-school study (3000 children and 141 pre-school settings) were that: (i) high-quality pre-school experience benefits children and these benefits remain evident at age 10; (ii) children made more gains in settings combining education and care and in nursery schools where there were more highly qualified staff; (iii) good early years staff provided direct teaching, instructive learning environments and 'sustained shared thinking' to extend children's learning; and (iv) a high-quality early years home environment is associated with gains for children but what parents do is more important than who they are.

In TLRP's discussions, the juxtaposition of formal and informal learning came to signify debates about the influence of social context. This was sometimes represented in terms of bounded environments, often with the classroom or child at the core and with multiple contextual layers circling beyond. Another usage, adoption of which grew over time, saw context more in terms of ever-present interpolating factors that crossed boundaries rather than being constrained by them. In this respect, Cole's (1996) distinction was helpful between general uses of the term 'context' to denote 'that which surrounds us' and 'that which weaves us together'.[31] The latter usage was particularly illuminative in relation to the influence of new technology on learning.

TLRP's work on technology began modestly with a single project on the integration of ICT into everyday classroom practices. The InterActive Education project (P8) worked with primary and secondary school teachers to study how subject knowledge could be enhanced through the use of new technologies. The use of mobile and other forms of technology is now so pervasive and so embedded within the cultures of children and young people that it provides a very strong illustration of the knowledge and experiential resources that exist beyond formal educational settings. Such knowledge is, however, somewhat idiosyncratic and uneven, making it a difficult resource to harness in schools. The project found that technology could be particularly effective at enhancing subject knowledge when teachers were able to bridge between the idiosyncratic and the intended curricular learning using tailored software. The software was seen, in sociocultural terms, as a mediating tool in support of the teaching–learning process. A similar conclusion was reached in a supplementary early years technology project in Scotland – InterPlay (P1). In this work, the 'guided interaction' of teachers and young children was seen as crucial in supporting dispositions to learn through the use of new technologies – including electronic toys and devices of many sorts, as well as technologies designed for more conventional educational processes. (See Box 3, above, for more detail of these projects.)

In 2007, TLRP was able to launch a completely new phase of investigation on Technology Enhanced Learning with the joint backing of two UK Research Councils and an additional £12 million in funding. Known as TLRP-TEL and under the leadership of Richard Noss, this phase of work has developed its own momentum and will run to the end of 2012. Following a development phase, eight major projects were selected for investment. Thematic analysis on flexibility, inclusion, personalisation, productivity and capacity building was built in from the start (see www.tlrp.org/tel – accessed May 17, 2011). This thematic work is conclusively demonstrating the experiential power of new technology and its influence on learning, and also the fact that such phenomena are fast moving with high potential for penetrating conventional forms of educational provision. The new world of technological learning and experience is thus both a fantastic resource and a considerable threat to schooling practices as they have been understood in the past.

The InterActive Education projects synoptic book (Sutherland, Robertson, and John 2009) reflects on this in terms of its implications for school contexts. In this book Robertson and Dale write that there is a 'tendency to view schools as islands, loosely connected to society. … What young people learn in other places and spaces has little currency in the classroom … and … schools are represented as enduring features of the landscape, immune to change' (155). They suggest that schools reflect an 'assemblage' of social relations, assumptions and organisational arrangements with significant effects on pupils, teachers, parents and others. Change, they suggest, is inevitable, as the impact of new technology and of learning beyond school accumulates. The book concludes: 'Maybe it is time to consider young people's out-of-school knowledge and cultures not as 'distractions' from the main business of schooling, but as rich, complex, diverse and powerful sources for learning and as an important place to start in designing education for the twenty-first century' (176).

Teachers and policies (principles 9 and 10)

A distinctive characteristic of TLRP schools projects was their aim to generate new knowledge about effective teaching and learning in authentic settings, i.e. in classrooms led by teachers. In almost all cases this encouraged them to work directly with teachers, or other education professionals in classrooms, to *develop* innovations.[32] This contrasts with much existing research on 'what works', especially from the United States, which tends to rely on university-based researchers to develop and test interventions in quasi-experimental settings. Under this system, those programmes, projects and products that achieve respectable effect sizes are disseminated through, for example, the What Works Clearinghouse.[33] However, the transformation of evidence-based knowledge into sustainable and effective practice cannot be taken for granted. Promising innovations often fail simply because they are not implemented; and implementation depends on those who work on a daily basis with pupils taking ownership of new ideas and practices. This requires teacher learning.[34]

The premise from which TLRP started made investigation of teacher learning an integral part of the work of most projects. Therefore, almost all projects contributed some evidence to underpin TLRP Principle 9:

> *Principle 9: effective pedagogy depends on the learning of all those who support the learning of others.* The need for lecturers, teachers, trainers and co-workers to learn continuously in order to develop their knowledge and skill, and adapt and develop their roles, especially through practice-based inquiry, should be recognised and supported.

Much debate has centred on the issue of whether teachers need to learn new techniques or whether the ideas underpinning them are more important. Some argue (e.g. Webb et al. 2004) that changing practices can lead to changes in beliefs; others (e.g. Ajzen and Fishbein 1980) take the view that changing behaviour depends on changing beliefs because they provide the necessary reasons to act. The general conclusion, to be drawn from the diverse studies in TLRP, is that changes in behaviour and beliefs are both necessary and should be developed together, progressively. Furthermore, effective pedagogy depends not only on behavioural change and the acquisition of new knowledge but on the development of values and dispositions, and reappraisal of roles and relationships in and beyond the classroom. Such learning by teachers takes place in the workplace, through participation in collaborative activities with other 'insiders', although the involvement of outsiders, such as researchers, and the provision of well-researched materials can be highly valued.

These conclusions began to emerge early in the life of TLRP. During a mini-conference held in 2002, which brought together the first projects to conclude their work, researchers with very different interests (P4, P7, P10, P11 and P19) discovered that they all had findings regarding teacher learning. These were initially fleshed out in a BERA conference symposium and then published in a special issue of the journal, *Research Papers in Education* (volume 20, number 2, June 2005*)*. The editorial to this issue summarised the common themes:

(1) Learning is both individual and collective and involves both the acquisition of knowledge and skills and participation in social processes. Thus the development of supportive professional cultures within which teachers can learn is vitally important. Within schools, especially secondary schools, the focus is often the department or team. However, the very cohesion of these groups can create insularity and inhibit change. Dynamic and expansive learning environments need to provide opportunities for boundary crossings, which encourage teachers to learn from others in different networks or communities of practice.

(2) Teachers are most ready to accept ideas for change if they resonate with their existing or previous beliefs and experience. However, this does not make them right or appropriate. Teachers need to develop the knowledge and skills to evaluate evidence and the confidence to challenge taken-for-granted assumptions, including their own. This is difficult and it is often helpful to involve outsiders, perhaps researchers from universities or visiting teachers from other schools, in helping teachers to see things differently. Teachers need to be assured that it is acceptable and often fruitful to take risks. Trust is therefore of the essence.

(3) Evidence from research about effective practice is not always sufficiently accessible for teachers to use as a basis for action. Findings often need to be transformed into practical and concrete strategies that they can try out. This may involve the production of concise and user-friendly materials written in natural language although ideas are often mediated best by talk and personal contacts with other teachers who have had some success in using them. Researchers have a responsibility to communicate their work in accessible ways but other education professionals can also have an effective role in mediation of this kind. (James 2005, 107–8)

All the studies described in Box 9 above, emphasise the importance of interactions among teacher factors (e.g. knowledge, attitudes and behaviour), cultural factors (e.g. professional networks or communities) and structural factors (e.g. policy contexts).

Box 9

Evidence from school projects

One study in the network of projects, Improving Incentives in the Workplace (P19), investigated secondary school teachers' learning as a special case of workplace learning. Drawing on a wide literature, including analysis of metaphors of learning and sociocultural theory, Hodkinson and Hodkinson (2005) draw attention to the way teachers learn through individual activity, collective activity and planned activity. They argue that the current policy context in England restricts teachers' capacity to learn and that genuine improvements are only likely to come if more expansive learning environments are created in which teachers can learn through participation in a supportive learning culture.

Similar concerns with structural and dispositional barriers and affordances are raised in the article by Howes et al. (2005), who report work of the TLRP network of projects, Understanding and Developing Inclusive Practices in Schools (P11). Inclusive practices are defined as those that help to overcome barriers to participation and learning. The project was committed to institutional change, at the cultural level. Nevertheless, teacher learning was seen as central to this and, as a social process, has to proceed in a research-like way with the construction of alternative perspectives that can pose questions and disturb taken-for-granted assumptions. The researchers call these *interruptions* to thinking and practice. Outsiders, including researchers or teachers visiting from other schools, are an important resource because they can help to 'make the familiar strange' and encourage 'boundary crossing'. However, it requires determined leadership to maintain risky learning dialogues that can bring about change.

The importance of learning dialogues, particularly around what pupils can tell teachers about teaching and learning, was the central theme of the network of projects, Consulting Pupils about Teaching and Learning (P10). In this study the researchers were interested in whether teachers learned from pupils in a way that led to sustained changes in their practices. McIntyre, Pedder, and Rudduck (2005) produced evidence of both comfortable and uncomfortable learnings for teachers. They conclude that in order for teachers to change their practice a number of conditions are necessary: teachers need to believe that pupil perspectives are important; teachers need to help pupils to learn to take on the new roles demanded by consultation; teachers need to be confident that they can combine responding to the needs of government and to the views of pupils; teachers need support from school managers to develop regular ways of consulting pupils.

One of four studies within the network of projects, Towards Evidence-based Practice in Science Education (EPSE) (P7) explored factors that promote and inhibit the impact of educational research on teachers' practice. Ratcliffe et al. (2005) found that use of research evidence in the classroom depends on two factors: (i) the 'translation' or 'transformation' of research findings into tangible outputs such as teaching materials and (ii) the existence of a professional culture in the school that encourages teachers to explore ways to use research in practice. Teachers engaged more readily with research generated by others once they had some experience of doing research themselves. However, when judging whether a piece of educational research might cause them to change their practice, it was not the quality of the research, but the extent to which it accorded with their own existing practices and beliefs, that influenced them. This sometimes caused them to dismiss research findings that challenged their assumptions.

Teachers were also more inclined to pay attention to research disseminated through oral communication and personal contacts than written reports. The influence of research on practice was often indirect or mediated. This study concluded that if research findings are to make an impact on classroom practice they need to: produce *convincing* findings, which *resonate* with teachers' professional experience, and *translate* into practical strategies that are widely disseminated through *professional networks*.

An attempt at this kind of translation, or 'transformation', of research evidence into teacher practice was attempted in the project, The Role of Awareness in the Teaching and Learning of Literacy and Numeracy in Key Stage 2 (P4). Hurry et al. (2005) were particularly interested in: the relationship between teachers' knowledge and understanding of morphology; whether this awareness was reflected in their practice; and whether this was associated with gains in their pupils' spelling. The study concluded that research can be transformed into teacher practice but there are difficulties in sustaining professional development. Again, the policy context was seen to be crucial and provision of documentation alone is insufficient to ensure implementation.

As further TLRP projects reported their findings, these insights were elaborated, refined and expanded. Teacher-research, action research, practice-based enquiry or lesson study were regarded as key professional learning activities and many projects incorporated these in their design.

Underlying the examples given in Box 10 are some deeper questions about the purpose and value of action research and collaborative enquiry. These relate to earlier

Box 10

Evidence from school projects

Understanding and Developing Inclusive Practices in Schools (P11), which is described in the previous box (Box 9), was a collaborative action-research project in three local authorities. It addressed the question of how schools can include all children from the communities they serve and enable them both to participate fully and achieve highly. This project gave rise to an 'extension' project in Wales, Prosiect Dysgu Cydradd (or Facilitating Teacher Engagement in more Inclusive Practice) (P9). This project was built on evidence that many teachers remain unconvinced of the principle of inclusion. Through action research, it set out to draw more secondary teachers into the challenge of engaging all of their pupils in learning. A major innovation was the involvement of educational psychologists acting as facilitators to support and challenge. The project team found that: (i) many secondary school teachers are unfamiliar with action research and, unless they develop a sense of ownership, they see this approach to development as just another imposition; (ii) however, energy and creativity are released when teachers allow or invite their assumptions about pupils and learning to be challenged; and (iii) both school leaders and external facilitators (such as educational psychologists) have a role in providing support and challenge. One strong conclusion was that the process of reflection and action needs to be protected from external agenda.

The Learning How to Learn in Classrooms, Schools and Networks project (LHTL) (P13) was principally concerned with the conditions in schools and networks that would enable the positive effects of assessment for learning (AfL) to be scaled up and sustained without intensive and expensive support. This project investigated a 'logic model for a causal argument' that linked classroom practice to teachers' own learning practices and school management practices. It found that: (i) classroom-focused enquiry by teachers is a key condition for promoting autonomous learning by pupils and that schools that embed AfL make support for professional learning a priority and (ii) educational networks are much talked about but little understood, and electronic tools for professional development purposes are not well used, however, the intellectual capital of schools can be built on the social capital developed through teachers' personal networking practices. Therefore, school leaders need to create the structures and cultures that support collaborative classroom enquiry and the sharing of innovations in classroom practice, within and beyond the school, because a key aspect of teacher learning is 'knowledge creation'.

Linked to this project was a TLRP Research Training Fellowship, awarded to Pete Dudley, to undertake an investigation of ways in which Japanese Lesson Study might be adapted and used in UK schools.[35] This provides a formal approach to collaborative classroom enquiry that emerged as a crucial factor in the LHTL project. Teachers work in groups to formulate hypotheses about adjustments to lessons to improve learning. These are tested in Research Lessons that colleagues observe and discuss subsequently. New hypotheses and adjustments are tested in further iterations until the teachers feel ready to perform a public research lesson. The findings, which will be reported in a Ph.D. thesis, are that: (i) Research Lesson Study engages teachers at all levels of experience and sustains their interest over time; (ii) it involves pupils directly in the analysis of teaching; and (iii) leads to innovation in lesson design and improvements in pupil achievements.

discussion about learning in general – about whether learning is an individual or a social process, and what and whose ends it serves. Such issues were also explored in, Changing Teacher Roles, Identities and Professionalism (C-TRIP) (T5), one of TLRP's most successful thematic seminar series. These seminars invited presentation of new empirical and theoretical work and brought together two important traditions of enquiry about teachers' lives and practices: research that investigates *the social and policy contexts of teachers' lives* and research that focuses on the *enhancement of professional practice*.[36]

In his C-TRIP seminar paper, Elliott (2006) traces the concept of 'research-based teaching' in the UK to the work of Lawrence Stenhouse and his Humanities Curriculum Project in the late 1960s and early 1970s. He claims that Stenhouse had emancipatory intent:

Research-based teaching was viewed by Stenhouse as a form of research that focuses on overcoming the difficulties of achieving high-quality discussion in classrooms, given the norms that have traditionally shaped practice in them. For him, the transformation of the culture of teaching and learning that prevailed in the field of humanities education, and which he believed to be the primary source of students' disaffection, depends upon the capacity of teachers to adopt a research stance towards their practice. He did not view this capacity in purely individualistic terms. Cultural transformation depends on teachers collaborating together across classrooms and schools to identify and diagnose common problems they experience in attempting to realise the standards implied by the pedagogical aim of developing understanding – given that

their practice tends to be shaped by shared norms – and to devise experimental strategies for resolving them. Research-based teaching depends on the willingness of individual teachers to open up their practice to scrutiny by others. It therefore presupposes
the possibility of discerning shared problems and solutions in common across a wide
range of classroom contexts. (Elliott 2006, 3–4)

However, Elliott also perceives that the 'teachers as researchers' movement has
been re-shaped by the 'standards agenda'.

What is now known as 'practitioner research' tends to be understood as an inquiry
that may be carried out by individual teachers into how to drive up standards in
their classroom. [...]'Practitioner Research' of this kind is shaped by an objectivist
and instrumentalist rationality as opposed to the deliberative and democratic rationality embedded in the idea of research-based teaching to improve the ethical quality of teacher's interactions with students in the teaching–learning process. (Elliott
2006, 12)

Data from many TLRP projects indicated structural constraints on teachers' capacity
for professional learning that were not simply practical but 'an assault on values'
(Woods et al. 1997, 84). For example, approximately 80% of 1200 teachers sur-
veyed in the Learning How to Learn project (P13) reported marked gaps between
what they valued and what they practised. Most teachers believed more strongly in
promoting learning autonomy in their pupils than claimed to practise it; and they
practised 'performance orientation' more than they believed in its value (James
et al. 2007, 56). In-depth interviews with 37 teachers revealed that they felt constrained by the press for rapid 'curriculum coverage', 'teaching to the test' and a
'tick box culture'. Although values–practice gaps reduced significantly during the
course of the project, some remained. This poses a question about whether professionals who are able articulate educational values should be expected to tolerate
such levels of tension and dilemma in their professional lives. An optimistic mes-
sage from this project was that the 20% of teachers, who had most success in promoting AfL in their classrooms, were those who demonstrated a capacity for
strategic and reflective thinking and took responsibility for what happened in their
classrooms. They were not inclined to blame external circumstances or pupil characteristics but concentrated on the ways in which they could improve the learning
experiences for pupils (James et al. 2007, 215).

The character of teachers' professional lives was, as mentioned above, the other
strand of interest in the C-TRIP thematic seminar series (T5). It was also the particular focus of a TLRP associate project, Variations in Teachers' Work, Lives, and
their Effects on Pupils (VITAE) (P17). This longitudinal study of 300 teachers provided a new perspective on teachers' quality, retention and effectiveness over the
whole of their careers. The project found that: (i) pupils of teachers who are committed and resilient are likely to attain more than pupils whose teachers are not; (ii)
teachers' sense of positive professional identity is associated with well-being and
job satisfaction and this is a key factor in their effectiveness; (iii) the commitment
and resilience of teachers in schools serving more disadvantaged communities are
more persistently challenged than others; (iv) teachers do not necessarily become
more effective over time – a minority risk becoming less effective in later years;
and (v) sustaining and enhancing commitment and resilience is a key quality and
retention issue. The project concluded that strategies are needed for meeting the

needs of teachers in different phases in their professional lives, and in different communities. Furthermore, CPD may not be as influential as the work context in creating commitment, resilience and well-being in teachers. These factors are important in that they are correlated with pupil outcomes. This finding resonates with other TLRP research that looked beyond continuous professional development (CPD), as the main opportunity for teacher learning, to issues around recruitment, retention, initial teacher education (ITE) and induction.[37]

In England, the influential EPPE project (P2) found that the recruitment of highly qualified staff is the key factor in effective pre-school education. In Northern Ireland, Innovations for a Values-based Approach to Teacher Education project (P18), questioned the value of professional development activities. Focusing on the role of values in recruitment, ITE and induction, the project discovered that beginning teachers in Northern Ireland lacked diversity; few shared background with pupils, which made connection and communication difficult. This difficulty was compounded by the appointment of new teachers to temporary positions, which led to inconsistent induction. In Scotland, the Competence-based Learning in the Early Professional Development of Teachers project (P20) investigated informal identity formation in beginning teachers. As in the projects on pupil group work (see above), the emotional and relational aspects were found to be important in the early stages with role aspects, including cognitive learning, featuring later. Patterns of social interaction correlated with job satisfaction. The director of this project noted at the 2006 TLRP annual conference:

> Pupil engagement in learning and their sense of worth depend also on the personal qualities of new teachers and the gradual growth of relationships that are imbued with mutual trust and confidence. This reciprocity is important for the further development of teaching and learning.

Comparing teacher education across the four countries of the United Kingdom, a TLRP thematic group on Teaching and Learning Policy in Post-devolution UK Contexts (T7) found aspects of both convergence and divergence in grade structures, services, standards and structures.

All these studies suggest that the two strands of the C-TRIP seminar series are closely interrelated: the enhancement of professional practice is influenced by the social and policy context of teacher's lives. C-TRIP accumulated a very considerable body of evidence on the material significance of policy – connected with history, regional or national specificity and education phase or sector – which contributes to the case for TLRP's tenth principle:

> *Principle 10: effective pedagogy demands consistent policy frameworks with support for learning as their primary focus.* Organisational and system level policies need to recognise the fundamental importance of continual learning – for individual, team, organisational and system success – and be designed to create effective learning environments for all learners.

Most TLRP projects raised questions and produced evidence about the impact of policy at three levels – school, local authority and the nation – and the interactions among these levels.

At school level many researchers observed that when senior management support innovation it becomes sustainable. However, head teachers revealed their concerns about leading learning in their schools within the context of prescriptive government policy. For example, within the Learning How to Learn project (P13), Swaffield and MacBeath (2006) found that challenges for leadership include resolving tension between 'bottom-up' growth and 'top-down' mandated change. Yet it was those school management systems that prioritised developing a sense of purpose, supporting professional development, auditing expertise and supporting networking, that were significantly more effective in fostering learning how to learn in classrooms (James et al. 2007). Similarly, the Pupil Consultation project (P10) found that support and commitment of school leaders was vital to ensure that consultation led to transformation in pedagogic practice. The InterActive Education and the Interactive Teaching projects (P8, P16) also found that support for professional development, to help teachers develop expertise in using ICT in dialogic teaching, was as important as providing equipment and technical training in its use.

Amongst TLRP project teams there was sometimes a perception that progress was being made despite government policy rather than because of it. However, there were exceptions. Some projects worked directly with policy makers to influence the policy agenda. The EPPE associate project, directly funded by the Department for Children, Schools and Families (formerly the Department for Education and Skills; now, since the 2010 election, the Department for Education), has been highly effective in influencing policy for pre-school. The Thinking Skills project (P5) worked with policy makers in Northern Ireland, in Wales and in some local authorities in England; larger-scale development projects have been rolled out as a result. The project on Intensive Quantities (P14) has had an impact on the Scottish curriculum for mathematics, as a result of direct contact. And the EPSE project (P7) has influenced the creation of the twenty-first century science GCSE, and the demise of the Key Stage 3 national tests in science, which overemphasised factual recall and under-emphasised conceptual learning and scientific literacy. However, anomalies and tensions remain and there is still much work to do to make policy better informed by research evidence. Building the social capital, to support meaningful activities and to ameliorate policy constraints on developing effective pedagogy, may be slightly easier in the smaller and more cohesive countries of the UK. But values are always contested in a democracy and challenges are likely to remain. What is important is that all those with an interest in effective pedagogy – pupils, parents, teachers, researchers, policy makers and the public at large –strive together to find and establish socially just policy frameworks that truly support learning for diverse learners.

At the beginning of this review, it was noted that the first version of TLRP's ten principles was presented graphically on an ellipse to indicate that they represent no firm linear hierarchy. However, the sequence reproduced here claims to possess a logic. Two later versions, adapted for higher education (David 2009) and workplace learning (Brown 2009), reverse the order. Thus, the TLRP principle related to policy frameworks comes first in these versions. This decision was partly influenced by a post-school project, Policy, Learning and Inclusion in the Learning and Skills Sector,[38] that investigated the impact of key national policy levers, such as funding, targets and inspection, on teaching, learning and assessment in the Learning and Skills System (LSS). After the 2006 TLRP annual meeting, when these principles were debated, this project team held a 'long discussion' and submitted a detailed commentary on the tenth principle, questioning its ordering. Among the points they made are two which have relevance beyond the LSS:

- Centralised control appears to be having the paradoxical effect of increasing the agency of tutors, precisely because a punitive audit culture and an excess of policy have forced them to consider their basic values and their professional stance.
- We agree with the conclusion of Seymour Sarason that teachers cannot create the conditions for students to become creative lifelong learners, if those conditions do not exist for the teachers.

The project team concluded (Coffield 2008, 25) that the skills sector would benefit from a 'social partnership' between government and other stakeholders with more local and collaborative decision-making. 'This would allow for more professional participation and feedback, making change more gradual and reflective.' This conclusion might equally apply to the schools sector.

The impact of TLRP's analysis of ten principles for effective pedagogy

There is enormous contemporary interest in forming judgements of the degree of impact, and thus value for money, of research investments in social science. TLRP reflected these concerns from its inception and was developed explicitly to make a difference. In academic terms this was justified through the Enlightenment tradition 'seeking improvement through the application of reason' (Pollard 2005) and the Programme has contributed significantly to thinking about evidence informed policy and practice within the UK (see Pollard and Oancea 2010).

In considering the actual impact of TLRP's 'ten principles', it is helpful to review the UK context at the time and also the strategies adopted for user engagement, knowledge transformation and distribution (T14). The ten principles, as framed in relation to teaching and learning in schools before the 2010 change of UK government, responded to a growing concern with pedagogy in schools. For example, an agenda known as *Every Child Matters* was introduced and backed by *National Strategies* for teaching and learning in England; a new *Curriculum for Excellence* was implemented in Scotland; teaching and learning was prioritised by *The Learning Country* and *Aiming for Excellence* in Wales; and Northern Ireland's *Curriculum Review* built on new understandings of how children learn, giving more freedom to teachers to respond to pupils' needs. The UK context was thus one in which there was growing awareness of the significance of the quality of teaching in enhancing learner outcomes – reinforced by reports both from OECD (2005) and McKinsey (Barber and Mourshed 2007) and by PISA's international comparisons (e.g. OECD 2007).

TLRP was established with, and sustained, an ambition to contribute to policy and practice. For this reason, all project investments were required to prioritise 'user engagement' at two levels. Teachers or other practitioners in specific research sites were involved in project research activity. In some cases, they simply advised but in others they participated as co-researchers – sometimes working towards higher degrees in the process. At the national level, projects were encouraged to enlist the support of organisations with the reputation, resources or role to offer 'high leverage' for the dissemination of findings. Thus government departments and agencies, charities, local authorities, pressure groups, etc, were informed and engaged throughout the research process. In these ways, practical credibility was enhanced and the potential for large-scale impact was established. These alliances between researchers and users were reinforced through project advisory groups and by inviting key users to attend project and cross-Programme events. Good relationships with major national user organisations in key sectors were also nurtured by the TLRP Directors' Team, working from its London base.[39]

TLRP project researchers distilled their findings through a small set of standard Programme outputs – including posters, research briefings and books in the TLRP series.[40] These were intended to provide accessible accounts of the research – thus delivering on the Programme ambition to combine relevance and quality. Such work was complemented by more academic work, often published in journal, conference or working papers.

As we have seen, by building on these project resources, the Programme team sought to synthesise, distil and transform this knowledge further through the device of the 'ten principles'. This was initially achieved through the TLRP Commentary *Improving Teaching and Learning* (James and Pollard 2006).

In 2007, with the encouragement of government departments and professional organisations, the representation of the principles was refined to become a pullout poster for use in school staff rooms. This was included in a magazine written primarily for teachers. 40,000 copies were distributed, including to all UK schools, together with a DVD of case studies and interviews, filmed in project schools, to illustrate the principles in practice (TLRP 2007).

This latter version was reproduced, in content if not in form, in several other papers and publications by the Programme Team, for example: in a 2007 paper for the Prime Minister's Strategy Team at the Cabinet Office; in an audit paper for a 2007 workshop with the Department of Children, Schools and Families' National Strategies Team; as Research Survey 2/4 for the Cambridge Primary Review in 2008; as an article entitled 'What have we learned from TLRP?' for a special issue of the National Union of Teachers' journal, *Education Review*, (volume 21, number 1, summer 2008, 90–100); in a response to the European Commission's Public Consultation on Schools for the twenty-first century. Members of the TLRP Directors' Team also spoke about the ten principles at a wide range of professional and academic events. The analysis was incorporated into one of the UK's established textbooks for teachers, *Reflective Teaching* (Pollard 2008) and rolled out in tailored versions in TLRP Commentaries for Further Education (Brown 2009) and Higher Education (David 2009) with the support of related sectoral organisations.

The analysis has been taken up independently by other bodies. For example, it was distributed as a bilingual poster issued in the Welsh Assembly Government's *Curriculum and Assessment Update*, spring 2008. It was the focus of a series of articles in *Termtalk*, the newsletter of the General Teaching Council for Northern Ireland and in *Teaching Scotland,* the newsletter of the General Teaching Council for Scotland. The argument foregrounding the role of evidence-informed professional judgement was taken up by the General Teaching Council for England and led to co-publication of a TLRP Commentary on *Professionalism and Pedagogy* in which the principles underpinned proposals for a conceptual framework demarcating teacher expertise (Pollard 2010).

The analysis of ten principles was used for synoptic, summarising purposes in both the final Report of the Cambridge Primary Review (Alexander 2010, 302–3) and the UK Government's 2008 Foresight Programme Report on mental capital and well-being (Feinstein, Vorhaus, and Sabatanes 2008). It was promoted for teachers by the University Council for Teacher Education, at its 2008 conference, and by the Teacher Development Agency through its Teacher Training Resource Bank. Teacher training courses in many parts of the UK began to use the analysis (for an example, see Barber 2009).

By May 2009, when the generic phase of TLRP formally ended, the pdf of the 2006 *Improving Teaching and Learning in Schools* commentary, in which the first version of the principles was published, had been downloaded 225,399 times. The later version in the *Principles into Practice* magazine had been downloaded 85,352 times. In terms of print, the 35,000 distribution of the 2006 Commentary was matched by that of the 2010 Commentary. In addition, the principles have featured in the newsletters of all UK General Teaching Councils, thus reaching some 500,000 teachers.

From the evidence cited above, we feel able to claim that TLRP's attempt to distil and synthesise diverse project findings into a coherent and accessible representation was successful at the level of engaging many of the key organisations that mediate between researcher, practitioner and policy maker communities. We see such engagement as being, in normal circumstances, a necessary condition for real impact on the ground.

However, we acknowledge the lack of hard evidence on the extent to which actual practice or actual policy has altered as a result of this work. We do, of course, have examples of such direct impact, but in most circumstances the role of research will be to provide evidence to be considered alongside many other factors. Influence is thus not likely to be direct or immediate.

More realistically, we prefer to see TLRP's work on ten principles in the sweep of history and as part of an international movement to accumulate knowledge about effective teaching, learning and educational provision. Progressively and incrementally, we would argue, more is being understood and evidenced about pedagogic effectiveness. Meta-analysis by scholars, such as Hattie (2009), is being complemented by programmatic enquiries in many countries – such as those of the commentators on this review.

Conclusion

In this contribution we have reviewed the origins and characteristics of TLRP's ten principles of effective teaching and learning and have provided illustrations of their evidential foundations. We have acknowledged the presentation of 'ten principles' as a summarising device to distil complexity and to contribute towards the quality of judgements by practitioners, policy makers and others.

The presentation of ten principles is TLRP's attempt to answer the question which was posed at the start of its funding: 'How can outcomes be improved for learners in all educational contexts and sectors across the UK?'. Such a question can only be answered in general terms and this we have tried to do. However, we are aware that other research groups, across the world, are wrestling with similar attempts to construct synoptic representations of their understanding.

International knowledge builds through exchange but must, in education, be applied with reference to the particular cultural, social, economic and political contexts of each country. Particular issues will thus be fore-grounded in relation to specific contexts, and different interpretations may be placed on some findings. Given contextual variations and the nature of education in relation to national futures and the distribution of opportunities, this is inevitable. However, a major responsibility for academics, we believe, is to look for commonalities. In this, we both join with Brian Simon in regretting the weakness of pedagogic awareness in England and align with international scholars in working towards global understanding.

Acknowledgements

We wish to express our gratitude and indebtedness to all those who have worked with us over the past ten years: to our colleagues in the TLRP Directors' Team; to the TLRP Steering Committee; to funders and staff at the ESRC who attempted to keep us on track; to all those involved as researchers or researched in the 100+ TLRP investments; and many, many more. Anything of value that may be found in this review is due, in large measure, to their ideas and efforts. However, the mistakes and misunderstandings are ours alone. Finally, we are hugely grateful to those, from across the world, who have taken the time to read and respond to this account. We hope that, together, we will stimulate a lively and continuing debate on issues at the heart of teaching and learning in schools, in the hope that we can make a difference.

Notes

1. TLRP's generic phase ran from 2000 to 2009. Some additional work on technology-enhanced learning (the TEL phase) completes in 2012.
2. Details of these outputs can be found on the TLRP website at: http://www.tlrp.org/pub/index.html and via the British Education Index at https://bei.leeds.ac.uk/freesearch/TLRP/BEISearch.html (accessed May 17, 2011).
3. See James 2006, for a detailed example drawing on the experience of one large project.
4. By the conclusion of the programme the balance had shifted and, by 2009, only approximately one-third of projects had focused on schools. The majority researched further and higher education, workplace and adult learning.
5. See http://www.tlrp.org/themes/index.html (accessed May 17, 2011).
6. This did not apply to 'associate projects', funded from other sources. Neither were research training fellowships formally evaluated because their principal output was expected to be a Ph.D. thesis which would be examined in the usual way.
7. The summary evaluation grades are given in Appendix A and a digest of evaluation comments can be found as appendices in the End of Award Report for the Programme 2002–2009: see http://www.tlrp.org/manage/progrep.html (accessed May 17, 2011).
8. The presentation and handout related to the session, 'Making sense of TLRP' can be found at http://www.tlrp.org/conference/2006/programme.html (accessed May 17, 2011).
9. For more information see: http://www.tlrp.org/themes/themes/tenprinciples.html
10. *Professionalism and Pedagogy: a contemporary opportunity,* published with the General Teaching Council for England, is available at: http://www.tlrp.org/pub/commentaries.html (accessed May 17, 2011).
11. The evidence for this can be found in the Annual and End of Award Reports of the first Programme Director, Charles Desforges (1999–2002). Accessible at: http://www.tlrp.org/manage/progrep.html (accessed May 17, 2011).
12. See, for example, Young (2008) who now takes a different (social realist) view from the one he promulgated 30 years earlier.
13. See http://www.tlrp.org/proj/phase11/phase2d.html (accessed May 17, 2011).
14. See 'Inspiring more teenagers to study science', *Nuffield Foundation Newsletter,* Issue 14, spring 2010, 1. Downloadable from www.nuffieldfoundation.org (accessed May 17, 2011).
15. Lave and Wenger. 1991 The references 'Lave and Wenger (1991) and Thorpe and Mayes (2010)' are cited in text but not provided in the reference list. Please provide the full reference details or delete them from the citation., might be the best example.

16. Both Sfard and Engeström contributed keynote addresses to the TLRP annual conference in 2004.

17. In preparation for discussions at the 2003 TLRP annual conference, all projects commissioned at that time were asked to produce a paper on their 'Conceptions of teaching and learning'.

18. In the first month of publication 38,000 copies were downloaded from the TLRP website, and within two years downloads numbered 213,170.

19. The text of these can be accessed at http://www.tlrp.org/themes/seminar/moon/papers. html (accessed May 17, 2011).

20. The participants involved in this thematic seminar series engaged with this model, critiqued it and built on it. The resulting papers were published in a special issue (vol. 18, no. 4) of *The Curriculum Journal* in 2007. Some authors were from TLRP projects, for example, the Evidence-based Practice in Science Education (EPSE) projects, but other contributions are from Germany and Denmark. These provide an important European perspective on these issues, which is less familiar in the UK than the work carried out in other Anglophone countries.

21. However, their discussion is more focused on the contextual demands of teacher learning, which will be revisited in relation to TLRP Principle 9.

22. The TLRP professional learning project on 'Vicarious Learning and Teaching of Clinical Reasoning Skills' developed multi-media resources to help scaffold learning. More detail is available at: http://www.tlrp.org/proj/phase111/cox.htm (accessed May 17, 2011).

23. See http://www.tlrp.org/proj/rtfbevan.html (accessed May 17, 2011) Robin Bevan's Ph. D. thesis, *From black boxes to glass boxes: the application of computerised concept mapping in schools*, is available in the University of Cambridge Faculty of Education Library.

24. Poor marking quality of Key Stage 3 national tests in England in the summer of 2008, contributed to the decision by Government to get rid of them.

25. GCSE – General Certificate of Secondary Education examinations; PIPS – Performance Indicators in Primary Schools System, see: http://www.cemcentre.org/RenderPage.asp? LinkID=22210000 (accessed May 17, 2011); ELLI – Effective Lifelong Learning Inventory, see: http://www.ellionline.co.uk/ (accessed May 17, 2011); ALCPS – Assessment of Learner Centered Practices, see (McCombs and Miller 2007).

26. See http://www.assessment-reform-group.org (accessed 17th May 2011).

27. The TLRP Learning How to Learn project team (P13) was consulted about this.

28. The survey sample of 5500 adults was drawn from the British Household Paned Survey, and this was combined with data from 120 interviews.

29. See website at: http://www.tlrp.org/proj/rtfbrookes.html (accessed May 17, 2011).

30. Evidence from the HSKE project, and its linked fellowship, focusing particularly on the social and emotional dimension of secondary transfer, was the focus of an innovative dramatic representation of research findings which is now available on a DVD (see http://www.tlrp-archive.org/cgi-bin/tlrp/news/news_log.pl?display=1181220375 for details).

31. See Thorpe and Mayes (2009) for a discussion of these representations.

32. The exception might be the literacy and numeracy projects (P4; P14) although the project on spelling using morphology carried out research on how the interventions developed by researchers could be transformed into teacher practice (Hurry et al. (2005)).

33. See http://ies.ed.gov/ncee/wwc/aboutus/ (accessed May 17, 2011).

34. In order to avoid cumbersome expression, 'teacher learning' is used in this article to encompass the learning of all adults who provide support for learning.

35. See http://www.tlrp.org/proj/phase111/rtfdudley.htm (accessed May 17, 2011) for details and publications.

36. In addition to a collection of seminar papers, it produced an annotated bibliography of 100 texts produced since January 2000, plus an appendix reviewing the literature prior to 2000. These can be downloaded from http://www.tlrp.org/themes/seminar/gewirtz/ (accessed May 17, 2011).

37. A substantial bibliography of 446 recent research publications on teacher education was compiled by the Teacher Education Group for the research resources section of the

TLRP website. This can be found at: http://www.tlrp.org/capacity/rm/wt/teg/ (accessed May 17, 2011).
38. See http://www.tlrp.org/proj/phase111/coffield.htm (accessed May 17, 2011).
39. For more information on such strategies, see http://www.tlrp.org/users/ (accessed May 17, 2011) or Pollard (2011).
40. See http://www.tlrp.org/manage/admin/outputnew.html (accessed May 17, 2011) for a full description of these and http://www.tlrp.org/pub (accessed May 17, 2011) for the published outcomes.

References

Ajzen, I., and M. Fishbein. 1980. *Understanding attitudes and predicting social behaviour.* Englewood Cliffs, NJ: Prentice Hall.

Alexander, R. 2001. *Culture and Pedagogy: International comparisons in primary education.* Oxford: Blackwell.

Alexander, R. 2004. Still no pedagogy? Principle, pragmatism and compliance in primary education. *Cambridge Journal of Education* 34, no. 1: 7–34.

Alexander, R. 2006. *Education as dialogue. Moral and pedagogical choices for a runaway world.* Hong Kong: HKIED in conjunction with Dialogos UK.

Alexander, R., ed. 2010. *Children, their world, their education: Final report and recommendations of the Cambridge Primary Review.* Abingdon: Routledge.

Assessment Reform Group (ARG). 2002. *Assessment for learning: 10 principles.* Cambridge: University of Cambridge, School of Education. http://www.assessment-reform-group.org/publications.html (Download in English, Welsh and Japanese).

Bakhtin, M. 1981. *The dialogic imagination,* ed. M. Holquist. Austin, TX: University of Texas Press.

Bakhtin, M. 1986. *Speech genres and other late essays*, ed. C. Emerson, and M. Holquist. Austin, TX: University of Texas Press.

Banks, F., J. Leach, and B. Moon. 1999. New understandings of teachers' pedagogic knowledge. In *Learners and pedagogy*, ed. J. Leach, and B. Moon, 89–110. London: Paul Chapman.

Barber, M., and M. Mourshed. 2007. *How the world's best performing schools systems come out on top*. London: McKinsey.

Barber, P. 2009. Putting principles at the core in teacher education. *TLRP Research Briefing no. 70*. London: TLRP, Institute of Education, University of London.

Bevan, R., D. Pedder, M. James, and P. Carmichael. 2007. From black boxes to glass boxes: On-screen learning in schools with concept maps. *TLRP Research Briefing no. 21*. London: TLRP, Institute of Education, University of London.

Biesta, G., J. Field, P. Hodkinson, F.J. Macleod, and I.F. Goodson. 2011. *Improving learning through the lifecourse*. London: Routledge.

Black, P., and D. Wiliam. 1998. Assessment and classroom learning. *Assessment in Education* 5, no. 1: 5–75.

Black, P., C. Harrison, C. Lee, B. Marshall, and D. Wiliam. 2003. *Assessment for learning: Putting it into practice*. Maidenhead: Open University Press.

Boaz, A., W. Solesbury, and F. Sullivan. 2004. *The practice of research reviewing 1: An assessment of 28 review reports*. London: ESRC UK Centre for Evidence-based Policy and Practice, Queen Mary College.

Bridges, D. 2009. Evidence based policy. What evidence? What basis? Whose policy? *TLRP Research Briefing no. 74*. London: TLRP, Institute of Education, University of London..

Bridges, D., and M. Watts. 2008. Educational research and policy: Epistemological considerations. *Journal of Philosophy of Education* no. 42, Special Issue, Supplement 1: 41–62.

Brown, A. 2009. *Higher skills development at work. A commentary by the teaching and learning research programme*. London: TLRP, Institute of Education, University of London.

Chevallard, Y. 1991. *La Transposition Didactique: du savoir savant au savoir en-seigne* [Didactic transpositions: From produced knowledge to taught knowledge]. Paris: La Pensee Sauvage.

Coffield, F. 2008. FE needs more partnership and collaboration in decision making. In *Challenge and change in further education. A commentary by the teaching and learning research programme*, ed. I. Nash, S. Jones, K. Ecclestone, and A. Brown, 24–5. London: TLRP, Institute of Education, University of London.

Cole, M. 1996. *Cultural psychology: A once and future discipline*. Cambridge, MA: Belknap.

Crozier, G., D. Reay, and J. Clayton. 2009. The socio-cultural and learning experiences of working class students in higher education. In *Widening participation in higher education*, ed. M. David, 16–7. London: Routledge.

Daugherty, R. 2009. Assessment of significant learning outcomes. *TLRP Research Briefing no. 75*. London: TLRP, Institute of Education, University of London.

David, M. 2009. *Effective learning and teaching in higher education. A commentary by the teaching and learning research programme*. London: TLRP, Institute of Education, University of London.

Department for Children, Schools, Families (DCSF). 2008. *The assessment for learning strategy*. Nottingham: DCSF.

Dunbar, K., J. Fugelsang, and C. Stein. 2007. Do naïve theories ever go away?. In *Thinking with data: 33rd carnegie symposium on cognition*, ed. M. Lovett, and P. Shah. Mahwah, NJ: Erlbaum.

Dweck, C. 1999. *Self-theories: Their role in motivation, personality and development*. Philadelphia, PA: Psychology Press.

Ecclestone, K., G. Biesta, and M. Hughes, eds. 2010. *Transitions and learning through the lifecourse*. London: Routledge.

Edwards, A. 2005. *Cultural historical activity theory and learning: A relational turn*. TLRP annual conference keynote address, November, in University of Warwick, England.

Edwards, R., G. Biesta, and M. Thorpe, eds. 2009. *Rethinking contexts for learning and teaching*. London: Routledge.

Elliott, J. 2006. Research-based teaching. Paper given at TLRP C-Trip seminar. *The impact of research on professional practice and identity*, April, in King's College London, England.

Engeström, Y. 1999. Activity theory and individual and social transformation. In *Perspectives on activity theory*, ed. Y. Engeström, R. Miettinen, and R.-L. Punamaki, 19–38. Cambridge: Cambridge University Press.

Feinstein, L., D. Budge, J. Vorhaus, and K. Duckworth. 2008. *The social and personal benefits of learning: A summary of key research findings*. London: Institute of Education, University of London.

Feinstein, L., J. Vorhaus, and R. Sabates. 2008. *Foresight mental capital and wellbeing project. Learning through life: Future challenges*. London: The Government Office for Science.

Field, J. 2010. Foreword. In *Transitions and learning through the lifecourse*, ed. K. Ecclestone, G. Biesta, and M. Hughes. London: Routledge.

Filer, A., and A. Pollard. 2000. *The social world of pupil assessment in primary school*. London: Continuum.

Gardner, H. 1983. *Frames of mind: The theory of multiple intelligences*. New York: Basic Books.

Gardner, H. 1991. *The unschooled mind*. New York: Basic Books.

Gardner, H. 1992. A response. *Teachers' College Record* 94, no. 2: 407–13.

Galton, M. 2010. *Assessing group work*. 3rd. ed. *International encyclopedia of education*. Vol. 3. Oxford: Elsevier.

Hattie, J. 2009. *Visible learning: A synthesis of over 800 meta-analyses relating to achievement*. London: Routledge.

Hodkinson, H., and P. Hodkinson. 2005. Improving schoolteachers' workplace learning. *Research Papers in Education* 20, no. 2: 109–31.

Howard-Jones, P. 2007. *Neuroscience and education: Issues and opportunities*. London: TLRP, Institute of Education, University of London.

Howes, A., T. Booth, A. Dyson, and J. Frankham. 2005. Teacher learning and the development of inclusive practices and policies: Framing and context. *Research Papers in Education* 20, no. 2: 133–48.

Hughes, M. 2006. Home-school knowledge exchange. *Educational Review* 58, no. 4: 385–47.

Hurry, J., T. Nunes, P. Bryant, U. Pretzlik, M. Parker, T. Curno, and L. Midgley. 2005. Transforming research on morphology into teacher practice. *Research Papers in Education* 20, no. 2: 187–206.

Ivanic, R., R. Edwards, D. Barton, M. Martin-Jones, M. Fowler, B. Hughes, G. Mannion, K. Miller, C. Satchwell, and J. Smith. 2009. *Improving learning in college: Rethinking literacies across the curriculum*. London: Routledge.

James, D., and G. Biesta. 2007. *Improving learning cultures in further education*. London: Routledge.

James, M. 2005. Introduction: Insights on teacher learning from the Teaching and Learning Research Programme (TLRP). *Research Papers in Education* 20, no. 2: 105–8.

James, M. 2006. Balancing rigour and responsiveness in a shifting context: Meeting the challenges of educational research. *Research Papers in Education* 21, no. 4: 365–80.

James, M., P. Black, P. Carmichael, C. Conner, P. Dudley, A. Fox, D. Frost, et al. 2006. *Learning how to learn: Tools for schools*. Abingdon: Routledge.

James, M., and S. Brown. 2005. Grasping the TLRP nettle: Preliminary analysis and some enduring issues surrounding the improvement of learning outcomes. *The Curriculum Journal* 16, no. 1: 7–30.

James, M., R. McCormick, P. Black, P. Carmichael, M.-J. Drummond, A. Fox, J. MacBeath, et al. 2007. *Improving learning how to learn: Classrooms, schools and networks*. Abingdon: Routledge.

James, M., and A. Pollard. 2006. *Improving teaching and learning in schools*. London: TLRP, Institute of Education, University of London.

James, M., and A. Pollard. 2008. What have we learned from TLRP? *Education Review* 21, no. 1: 90–100.

James, M., and A. Pollard. 2009. Learning and teaching in primary schools: Insights from TLRP. In *The Cambridge primary review research surveys*, ed. R. Alexander, C. Doddington, J. Gray, L. Hargreaves, and R. Kershner. Abingdon: Routledge.

Kane, M. 2001. Concerns in validity theory. *Journal of Educational Measurement* 38, no. 4: 319–42.

Lave, J., and E. Wenger. 1991. *Situated learning: Legitimate peripheral participation.* Cambridge, MA: University of Cambridge Press.

Mansell, W., M. James, and the Assessment Reform Group. 2009. *Assessment in schools. Fit for purpose? A commentary by the teaching and learning research programme.* London: TLRP, Institute of Education, University of London.

Marshall, B., and M.-J. Drummond. 2006. How teachers engage with assessment for learning: Lessons from the classroom. *Research Papers in Education* 21, no. 2: 133–49.

McCombs, B., and L. Miller. 2007. *Learner-centred classroom practices and assessment: Maximizing student motivation, learning and achievement.* Thousand Oaks, CA: Corwin.

McGuinness, C., N. Sheehy, C. Curry, A. Eakin, C. Evans, and P. Forbes. 2006. Building thinking skills in thinking classrooms. ACTS (Activating Children's Thinking Skills) in Northern Ireland. *TLRP Research Briefing no. 18.* London: TLRP, Institute of Education, University of London.

McIntyre, D., D. Pedder, and J. Rudduck. 2005. Pupil voice: Comfortable and uncomfortable learning's for teachers. *Research Papers in Education* 20, no. 2: 149–68.

OECD. 2005. *Teachers matter: Attracting, developing and retaining effective teachers.* Paris: OECD.

OECD. 2007. *PISA 2006 science competencies for tomorrow's world.* Paris: OECD.

Pollard, A. 1982. A model of classroom coping strategies. *British Journal of Sociology of Education* 3, no. 1: 19–37.

Pollard, A. 2005. Taking the initiative? TLRP and educational research. *Educational Review.* Guest Lecture, October 12, School of Education, University of Birmingham, England. http://www.tlrp.org/dspace/handle/123456789/380 (accessed May 17, 2011).

Pollard, A. 2008. *Reflective teaching.* 3rd ed. London: Continuum.

Pollard, A., ed. 2010. *Professionalism and pedagogy: A contemporary opportunity. A TLRP commentary.* London: GTCE/TLRP.

Pollard, A. 2011. Exploring strategies for impact: Riding the wave with the TLRP. In *Knowledge mobilization and educational research: Politics, languages and responsibilities*, ed. L. Farrell and T. Fenwick. London: Routledge.

Pollard, A., and A. Filer. 1999. *The social world of pupil career.* London: Continuum.

Pollard, A., and A. Filer. 2007. Education, schooling and learning for life. *TLRP Research Briefing no. 23.* London: TLRP, Institute of Education, University of London.

Pollard, A., and A. Oancea. 2010. *Unlocking learning? Towards evidence-informed policy and practice in education. Final Report of the UK strategic forum for research in education.* London: British Educational Research Association (BERA).

Putnam, R. 1993. Prosperous community: Social capital and public life. *The American Prospect* 3, no. 13: 11–8.

Ratcliffe, M., H. Bartholomew, V. Hames, A. Hind, J. Leach, R. Millar, and J. Osborne. 2005. Evidence-based practice in science education: The researcher-user interface. *Research Papers in Education* 20, no. 2: 169–86.

Rudduck, J., and D. McIntyre. 2007. *Improving learning by consulting pupils.* London: Routledge.

Schuller, T., J. Preston, C. Hammond, A. Brassett-Grundy, and J. Bynner. 2004. *The benefits of learning: The impact of education on health, family life and social capital.* London: Routledge.

Sfard, A. 1998. On the two metaphors of learning and the dangers of choosing just one. *Educational Researcher* 27, no. 2: 4–13.

Shotter, J. 1993. *The cultural politics of everyday life.* Buckingham: Open University Press.

Shulman, L.S. 1986. Those who understand: Knowledge growth in teaching. *Educational Research Review* 57, no. 1: 4–14.

Simon, B. 1981. Why no pedagogy in England?. In *Education in the eighties: The central issues*, ed. B. Simon and W. Taylor. London: Batsford.

Stenhouse, L. 1975. *An introduction to curriculum research and development*. London: Heinemann.

Stephen, C., and L. Plowman. 2008. Enhancing learning with ICT in pre-school. *Early Child Development and Care* 178, no. 6: 637–54.

Swaffield, S., and J. MacBeath. 2006. Embedding learning how to learn in school policy: The challenge for leadership. *Research Papers in Education* 21, no. 2: 201–15.

Sutherland, R., S. Robertson, and P. John. 2009. *Improving classroom learning with ICT*. London: Routledge.

Sylva, K., E. Melhuish, P. Sammons, and I. Siraj-Blatchford. 2010. *Early childhood matters*. London: Routledge.

Thorpe, M., and T. Mayes. 2009. The implications of learning contexts for pedagogical practice. In *Rethinking contexts for learning and teaching*, ed. R. Edwards, G. Biesta, and M. Thorpe. London: Routledge.

TLRP. 2007. *Principles into practice: A teacher's guide to research evidence on teaching and learning*. London: TLRP, Institute of Education, University of London.

Torrance, H., and J. Sebba. 2007. Reviewing reviews: Towards a better understanding of the role of research reviews. *TLRP Research Briefing no. 30*. London: TLRP, Institute of Education, University of London.

United Nations. 1989. *Convention on the rights of the child*. New York: United Nations.

Verret, M. 1975. *Le Temps des Etudes* [Time and study]. Paris: Librarie Honore Champion.

Webb, R., G. Vulliamy, S. Hämäläinen, A. Sarja, E. Kimonen, and R. Nevalainen. 2004. A comparative analysis of primary teacher professionalism in England and Finland. *Comparative Education* 40, no. 1: 83–107.

Wood, D., J. Bruner, and G. Ross. 1976. The role of tutoring in problem-solving. *Journal of Child Psychology and Psychiatry* 17: 89–100.

Woods, P., B. Jeffrey, G. Troman, and M. Boyle. 1997. *Restructuring schools, restructuring teachers: Responding to changes in primary schools*. Buckingham: Open University Press.

Young, M.F.D., ed. 1971. *Knowledge and control: New directions for the sociology of education*. London: Collier-Macmillan.

Young, M.F.D. 2008. *Bringing knowledge back in: From social constructivism to social realism in the sociology of education*. Abingdon: Routledge.

Appendix A: Projects and thematic work reviewed for this contribution

Projects

Early years projects

P1: INTERPLAY: PLAY, LEARNING AND ICT IN PRE-SCHOOL SETTINGS

Award: ESRC RES-139-25-0006, 2003–2006, £87k
PI: Lydia Plowman, University of Stirling
Website: http://www.tlrp.org/proj/phase111/Scot_extc.html
Evaluation Grade: Good

P2: EPPE 3-11: THE EFFECTIVE PRE-SCHOOL AND PRIMARY EDUCATION (EPPE 3-11) (A TLRP Associated Project)

Award: DFES and DCSF, 2003–2013
PI: Brenda Taggart, Institute of Education, University of London
Websites: http://eppe.ioe.ac.uk/http://www.tlrp.org/proj/phase111/AssocEPPE.htm

Primary education projects

P3: HOME-SCHOOL KNOWLEDGE EXCHANGE IN PRIMARY EDUCATION
Award: ESRC L139 25 1078, 2001–2005, £965k
PI: Martin Hughes, Graduate School of Education, University of Bristol
Websites: http://www.home-school-learning.org.uk
http://www.tlrp.org/proj/phase11/phase2e.html
Evaluation Grade: Outstanding

P4: THE ROLE OF AWARENESS IN TEACHING AND LEARNING LITERACY AND NUMERACY IN KEY STAGE 2
Award: ESRC L139251015, 2001–2004, £788k
PI: TerezinhaNunes, Oxford University
Website: http://www.tlrp.org/proj/phase11/phase2h.html
Evaluation Grade: Good

P5: SUSTAINABLE THINKING CLASSROOMS
Award: ESRCL139 25 1042, 2001–2004, £233k
PI: Carol McGuinness, Queens University Belfast
Website: http://www.tlrp.org/proj/phase11/phase2g.html
Evaluation Grade: Problematic

P6: SUPPORTING GROUPWORK IN SCOTTISH SCHOOLS: AGE AND THE URBAN/RURAL DIVIDE
Award: ESRCRES-139-25-0004, 2003–2004, £74k
PI: Donald Christie, University of Strathclyde
Websites: http://www.groupworkscotland.org/
http://www.tlrp.org/proj/phase111/Scot_extb.html
Evaluation Grade: Good

Secondary education projects

P7: TOWARDS EVIDENCE-BASED PRACTICE IN SCIENCE EDUCATION (A network of projects)
Award: ESRC L139251003, 2000–2003, £449k
PI: Robin Millar, University of York
Website: http://www.tlrp.org/proj/phase1/phase1bsept.html
Evaluation Grade: Good

P8: INTERACTIVE EDUCATION: TEACHING AND LEARNING IN THE INFORMATION AGE
Award: ESRC RES-139-25-1060, 2001–2004, £934k
PI: Ros Sutherland, Graduate School of Education, University of Bristol
Websites: http://www.interactiveeducation.ac.uk/
http://www.tlrp.org/proj/phase11/phase2i.html

Evaluation Grade: Good

P9: FACILITATING TEACHER ENGAGEMENT IN MORE INCLUSIVE PRACTICE
Award: ESRC RES-139-25-0160, 2005–2007, £122k including co-funding
PI: Sue Davies, Trinity College Carmarthen
Website: http://www.tlrp.org/proj/smbdavies.html
Evaluation Grade: Good

Across school phases projects

P10: CONSULTING PUPILS ABOUT TEACHING AND LEARNING (A network of projects)
Award: ESRCL13925 1006, 2000–2003, £425k
PI: Jean Rudduck, University of Cambridge
Websites: http://www.consultingpupils.co.uk/
http://www.tlrp.org/proj/phase1/phase1dsept.html
Evaluation Grade: Outstanding

P11: UNDERSTANDING AND DEVELOPING INCLUSIVE PRACTICES IN SCHOOLS (A network of projects)
Award: ESRCL13925 1001, 2000–2003, £444k
PI: Mel Ainscow, University of Manchester
Website: http://www.tlrp.org/proj/phase1/phase1asept.html
Evaluation Grade: Good

P12: IMPROVING THE EFFECTIVENESS OF PUPIL GROUPS IN CLASSROOMS
Award: ESRC L139 25 1046, 2001–2005, £1,006k
PI: Peter Blatchford, Institute of Education London
Websites: http://www.spring-project.org.uk/
http://www.tlrp.org/proj/phase11/phase2a.html
Evaluation Grade: Good

P13: LEARNING HOW TO LEARN: IN CLASSROOMS, SCHOOLS AND NETWORKS
Award: ESRCL139 25 1020, 2001–2005, £926k
PI: Mary James, University of Cambridge and Institute of Education London
Websites: www.learntolearn.ac.uk
http://www.tlrp.org/proj/phase11/phase2f.html
Evaluation Grade: Outstanding

P14: 5-14 MATHEMATICS IN SCOTLAND: THE RELEVANCE OF INTENSIVE QUANTITIES
Award: ESRC RES-139-25-0009, 2003–2005, £60k
PI: Christine Howe, Strathclyde University
Website: http://www.tlrp.org/proj/phase111/Scot_extd.html

Evaluation Grade: Good

P15: CONSULTING PUPILS ON THE ASSESSMENT OF THEIR LEARNING (CPAL)

Award: ESRCRES-139-25-0163, 2005–2007, £87k
PI: Ruth Leitch, Queen's University Belfast
Websites: http://www.cpal.qub.ac.uk/
http://www.tlrp.org/proj/leitch.html
Evaluation Grade: Outstanding

P16: THE USE OF ICT TO IMPROVE LEARNING AND ATTAINMENT THROUGH INTERACTIVE TEACHING

Award: ESRC RES-139-25-0167, 2005–2007, £115k
PI: Steve Kennewell, Swansea Metropolitan University
Websites: http://www.interactive-teaching.org.uk/
http://www.tlrp.org/proj/kennewell.html
Evaluation Grade: Good

P17: VARIATIONS IN TEACHERS' WORK, LIVES, AND THEIR EFFECTS ON PUPILS (VITAE) (A TLRP Associated Project)

Award: DFES, 2001–2006
PI: Christopher Day, School of Education, University of Nottingham
Website: http://www.tlrp.org/proj/cday.html
Evaluation Grade: N/A

Higher education projects

P18: INNOVATIONS FOR A VALUES-BASED APPROACH TO TEACHER EDUCATION

Award: ESRC RES-139-25-0152, 2005–2007, £126k
PI: Alan Smith, University of Ulster
Website: http://www.tlrp.org/proj/asmith.html
Evaluation Grade: Good

Workplace learning projects

P19: IMPROVING INCENTIVES TO LEARNING IN THE WORKPLACE (A network of projects)

Award: ESRC L139251005, 2000–2003, £473k
PI: Phil Hodkinson, University of Leeds (for the project relevant to the school sector)
Website: http://www.tlrp.org/proj/phase1/phase1csept.html
Evaluation Grade: Outstanding

P20: COMPETENCE-BASED LEARNING IN THE EARLY PROFESSIONAL DEVELOPMENT OF TEACHERS

Award: ESRC RES-139-25-0122, 2004–2008, £732k

PI: Jim McNally, University of Stirling
Websites: http://www.ioe.stir.ac.uk/research/projects/epl/index.php
http://www.tlrp.org/proj/phase111/mcnally.htm
Evaluation Grade: Good

Lifelong learning project

P21: IDENTITY AND LEARNING (A TLRP Associated Project)
Award: ESRC general large grants, 1998–2004
PI: Andrew Pollard, Institute of Education, University of London
Website: http://www.tlrp.org/proj/phase111/ILP.html
Evaluation Grade: Outstanding

Thematic work

T1: TEACHER LEARNING (2002–2004)
Convenor: Mary James, University of Cambridge

T2: IDENTIFYING LEARNING OUTCOMES (2003–2004)
Convenor: Mary James, University of Cambridge

T3: PERSONALISED LEARNING (2004)
Convenors: Andrew Pollard and Mary James, University of Cambridge

T4: NEUROSCIENCE, HUMAN DEVELOPMENT AND TEACHING (2005–2006)
Convenor: Paul Howard-Jones, University of Bristol

T5: CHANGING TEACHER ROLES, IDENTITIES AND PROFESSIONALISM (2005–2006)
Convenor: Sharon Gewirtz, King's College London

T6: SCIENCE EDUCATION IN SCHOOLS (2006)
Convenor: John Gilbert, University of Reading

T7: TEACHING AND LEARNING POLICY IN POST-DEVOLUTION UK CONTEXTS (2006–2007)
Convenor: Ian Menter, Glasgow University

T8: CURRICULUM AND DOMAIN KNOWLEDGE (2006–2007)
Convenors: Robert McCormick and Robert Moon, Open University

T9: ASSESSMENT OF SIGNIFICANT LEARNING OUTCOMES (2006–2007)
Convenor: Richard Daugherty, University of Cardiff

T10: SOCIAL DIVERSITY AND DIFFERENCE: RESEARCHING INEQUALITIES IN TEACHING AND LEARNING (2006–2007)

Convenor: Miriam David, Institute of Education London

T11: EPISTEMOLOGICAL BASIS OF EDUCATIONAL RESEARCH FINDINGS (2006–2007)
Convenor: David Bridges, University of Cambridge

T12: REVIEWING REVIEWS (2006–2007)
Convenor: Harry Torrance, Manchester Metropolitan University

T13: ASSESSMENT IN SCHOOLS (2008–2009)
Convenor: Mary James, University of Cambridge

T14: COMMUNICATION, IMPACT AND KNOWLEDGE TRANSFER (2004–2007)
Convenor: Andrew Pollard, Institute of Education London

T15: IMPACT OF SOCIAL, ECONOMIC, MEDICAL AND ENVIRONMENTAL FACTORS AND INTERVENTIONS ACROSS THE LIFECOURSE (2006–2007)
Convenor: Leon Feinstein, Institute of Education London

T16: CONTEXTS, COMMUNITIES AND NETWORKS (2005–2006)
Convenor: Richard Edwards, University of Stirling

T17: TRANSITIONS THROUGH THE LIFECOURSE: ANALYSING THE EFFECTS OF IDENTITY, AGENCY AND STRUCTURE (2006–2006)
Convenor: Kathryn Ecclestone, Oxford Brookes University

Pedagogy, didactics and the co-regulation of learning: a perspective from the French-language world of educational research

Linda Allal

Faculty of Psychology and Educational Sciences, University of Geneva, Switzerland

Since pedagogy is a key term in the Teaching and Learning Research Programme (TLRP) principles, it is of interest to examine the evolution of the concept of pedagogy in the French-language world of education, as well as the emergence of a new field of research called 'didactics'. Work on situated cognition provides a framework for defining co-regulation of learning in the classroom as resulting from the joint influence of student self-regulation and of regulation from other sources (teachers, peers, curriculum materials, assessment instruments, etc.). Several examples of research on this topic are mentioned. In conclusion, it is argued that the concept of co-regulation of learning can be seen as a way of linking the TLRP principles of scaffolding and of student engagement.

Introduction

The contribution by Mary James and Andrew Pollard appearing in this volume presents ten principles developed by the Teaching and Learning Research Programme (TLRP) on the basis of studies carried out in schools and other education centres throughout the UK. The authors have formulated an impressive, well-documented synthesis of the findings acquired from over 100 research projects involving researchers from a wide range of disciplines and practitioners working at all levels of the educational system. The result of this endeavour is an interlocking set of principles that are conceptually coherent and carefully formulated to reflect the evidence coming from the TLRP projects. The authors provide an overview of the theoretical and empirical foundations of each principle and give numerous references to publications and websites that the reader can consult in order to learn more about the methods and findings of the studies and the thematic contributions of the forums organised by the programme.

As requested for this collection, my comments will deal with how the review by James and Pollard resonates with the work conducted in my own scientific community. My reference is the French-language community of educational research and practice, within which I have worked for over 30 years and which includes France and the French-speaking regions of Belgium, Canada and Switzerland. I will first examine the concepts of pedagogy and didactics, as they have emerged and evolved in this context, and the implications for the TLRP proposals. I will then discuss a topic of my own research – the co-regulation of learning – and the links I see with the TLRP principles.

Pedagogy and didactics

Pedagogy is a key term in the TLRP principles. Each principle begins with the words 'Effective pedagogy...' and then states a requirement to be met to promote quality and equity in student learning. James and Pollard present several arguments for their choice of the term 'pedagogy', which has replaced the expression 'teaching and learning' used in earlier TLRP publications. Their main argument is that pedagogy 'expresses the *contingent relationship* between teaching and learning' (in this volume, 8). I can only agree that this relationship – which implies interdependency of teaching and learning – is at the heart of educational undertakings. It must be noted, however, that most definitions of pedagogy, including those of Simon (1981) and Alexander (2004), quoted by James and Pollard (in this volume, 3, 8), refer to the act of teaching and its attendant discourse without explicit mention of the processes of learning. Put succinctly, pedagogy is generally considered to be embodied in teachers' actions and ideas, rather than being focused on teacher–learner transactions.[1] The nature of these transactions will be explored further in the second section of my response to their work.

UK publications on education often suggest that elsewhere in Europe the concept of pedagogy is well established and well accepted. While this may be true in some countries, its presence has in fact become quite marginal in most of the French-speaking world. An essay on *Pédagogie* by my colleague Hameline (1998) traces the evolution of the concept from its origins in scholarly reflections (Montaigne, Rousseau, etc.) on the purposes and principles of education to its institutionalisation in the Normal schools (teacher training institutes) of the late nineteenth century as a form of moral philosophy aimed at uplifting and guiding teachers in their work with children. Pedagogical doctrines, formulated by Pestalozzi, Decroly, Montessori, Freinet and others, were characterised by principles formulated at a high level of generality, as well as by a strong focus on practical details of educational method. In the early twentieth century, prominent figures in the emerging social sciences attempted to redefine the foundations and orientations of pedagogy. The sociologist Durkheim (1911) proposed to consider pedagogy as a 'practical theory' situated in an intermediate zone between art and science, like medical and political theories. Claparède (1912), founder of the J.-J. Rousseau Institute in Geneva, argued that pedagogy could acquire legitimacy only by rigorous scientific grounding in psychology. This position, shared by many researchers and leaders in education, inaugurated the development of a new field – *psychopédagogie* – which became a mainstay of teacher training in Belgium, France, Quebec and Switzerland. Although it sought to apply empirical findings from developmental and educational psychology, psycho-pedagogy retained a general level of prescriptive discourse similar to that of pedagogy.

Subsequent disregard of *pédagogie* and of *psychopédagogie*, which accelerated towards the end of the 1970s, can be explained by several factors (Hameline 1998; Hofstetter 2010). One of the most important is the development of *Sciences de l'éducation* as an autonomous field of research that draws on insights from a multiplicity of disciplines (psychology, sociology, history, linguistics, economics...), but cannot be reduced to the application of any one or even several of these disciplines. In the Faculty of Psychology and Educational Sciences that grew out of the J.-J. Rousseau Institute in Geneva, the term pedagogy has nearly disappeared (in the 2010–2011 bachelor and master programmes, it appears in only two course titles[2]). There remains, however, a highly articulate spokesman for pedagogy in France, Philippe Meirieu, professor at the University of Lyon 2, whose website (www.meirieu.com) provides substantial documentation on the history of pedagogy, its conceptual, moral and pragmatic foundations, and the debates it continues to inspire.

The decline of pedagogy has been hastened, in the French-language world of education, by the emergence, in the late 1970s, of discipline-based didactics (*didactiques des disciplines*) focused on the subject-matters of teaching: language, mathematics, science, etc. (for summaries in English by two prominent didacticians, see Caillot 2007; Chevallard 2007). This development is alluded to by James and Pollard (in this volume, 19) in their discussion of the didactic transposition of academic disciplinary knowledge into school-subject knowledge. From the beginning, the developers of didactics (most of whom were specialists in academic disciplines) took a highly critical stance with respect to pedagogy, considering it to be an antiquated, overly general discourse that could provide no useful guidance for the teaching of specific subjects. The researchers in didactics have developed a coherent, well-integrated set of concepts. Starting with the definition of the didactical system as a triadic relation between teacher, student and knowledge, they have analysed the didactic transposition of knowledge and the embodiment of knowledge in classroom situations. Studies of the dynamics of interactions between teachers and learners have also come under scrutiny in work on the functioning (and the breakdowns) of the 'didactic contract', defined as a set of mutual and largely implicit expectations between teacher and students with respect to an object of knowledge. More recent work includes the conceptualisation of bodies of knowledge as 'praxeologies' that contain both a form of practice (types of tasks and corresponding techniques) and a discourse or theory about the practice in question, its aims, its rationale, its effectiveness (Chevallard 2007).

Despite the important differences between pedagogy and didactics, as developed in the French-language world of education, they share, I believe, one common feature. Empirical research on the processes of learning, and especially on learning outcomes, is rarely the focus of their investigations. Writings on pedagogy often refer to theories or conceptions of learning illustrated by selected observations, but they contain few in-depth analyses of the learning outcomes attained by students in ordinary classrooms. Research in didactics has stronger empirical grounding in the observation of classroom activities, but student learning is analysed primarily through vignettes and prototypical excerpts of classroom talk, sometimes through qualitative analyses of a few individuals' progression, while leaving unanswered the question: what did each student learn in the situation or series of situations that were observed?

Returning to the choice by James and Pollard to frame the TLRP principles in terms of effective 'pedagogy', I would like to express two concerns stemming from my experience in the French-language world of education. Use of the term pedagogy will probably not facilitate the dissemination of the TLRP work in educational circles in Belgium, France, Quebec and Switzerland, given the long and complex history of this concept and its present disparaged status. The choice of pedagogy may, however, be appropriate for communication with practitioners and policy-makers in the UK where the term is not encumbered by past usage and may be more easily accepted with the meaning that the TLRP principles seek to promote. A second concern is more fundamental. Because pedagogy, in its traditional and contemporary definitions, is more directly focused on teaching (its practice and its discourse) than on learning, there is the risk that what was long the hallmark of English-language research – careful empirical analysis of learning processes and outcomes – may be downplayed and possibly neglected. It would be a loss if classroom research in the UK, or elsewhere, no longer sought, in a systematic way, to answer to the question: what did each student learn in the situations and activities under investigation? The fact that it is often difficult and sometimes even impossible to answer this question does not diminish its importance at a theoretical and a practical level. My own preference would thus be to retain the more cumbersome expression 'teaching and learning' when formulating principles for goals, activities and practices in educational settings. I think this might improve the chances of keeping the contingent relationship between teaching and learning clearly in view.

Co-regulation of learning

The expression 'co-regulation of learning' refers to the joint influence of student self-regulation and of regulation from other sources (teachers, peers, curriculum materials, assessment instruments, etc.) on student learning (Allal 2007). One could also define it as: processes of learning and of teaching that produce learning. The focus is thus on learning as the outcome of education and teaching is subsumed within the 'co' of 'co-regulation' (an approach which may not of course satisfy proponents of pedagogy and didactics who are interested chiefly in teaching). I will attempt to describe the emergence of this concept in French-language publications and its possible links with the TLRP principles.[3]

The regulation[4] of learning has long been an important topic in French-language publications in psychology and education. In his theory of cognitive development, Piaget (1975) defined the processes of regulation that explain how equilibration works and thereby allows the transformation of cognitive structures and the adaptation of behaviour in interaction with the environment. This focus on internal processes of *self*-regulation has continued to characterise contemporary research dealing with metacognitive and motivational dimensions of regulation. In contrast, researchers using concepts developed by Vygotsky (1978) have been concerned primarily with the regulation of learning that results from the interactive guidance provided by a tutor or teacher and from the use of tools that mediate the processes of learning. For example, in the didactics of French language instruction developed by Dolz and Schneuwly (1996), different text *genres* are considered to be tools – in the Vygotskian sense – for organising and regulating students' progression in oral and written text production. French-language research on assessment, and particularly on formative assessment (Allal 2010; Allal & Mottier Lopez 2005), has been influenced by both the Piagetian and Vygotskian conceptions of regulation. Considerable attention has been given to the ways in which various forms of self-assessment can activate the processes of metacognitive regulation (goal setting, monitoring, interpretation of feedback, adaptation of goal-directed behaviour), as well as to the regulations fostered by interactive assessment (e.g. student–teacher conferences) and by assessment tools (e.g. rubrics for peer and self-assessment, guidelines for constructing a portfolio) used in the classroom.

The perspective of situated cognition, particularly as elaborated by Cobb, Gravenmeijer, Yackel, McClain, and Whiteneck (1997), provides a framework for understanding the relations between active individual construction of knowledge and social processes of enculturation within a teaching/learning community. This framework offers a basis for postulating a reflexive relationship between student self-regulation and the regulations linked to various aspects of the teaching/learning context: namely, the structure of the learning activities, the transactions between students and the teacher, the exchanges among students, the tools embedded in the activities (Allal 2007). A reflexive relationship implies that processes of self-regulation govern students' engagement (or lack of engagement) with the affordances present in the teaching/learning context and that these affordances, in turn, support and constrain (or sometimes fail to support and constrain) students' self-regulation. Put more simply: it is postulated that the progression of student learning results from a process of co-regulation that entails interdependency between self-regulation and socially mediated forms of regulation.[5]

In order to study the co-regulation of student learning in the classroom, the most obvious situations are those involving one-to-one or small-group interactions in which the behaviour of each actor (student, teacher) is directly contingent on that of the other(s). But what about collective lessons, in which the teacher interacts with an entire class? Since this remains the most widespread format of teaching, it is important to understand how co-regulation may or may not occur when the teacher interacts with a large group of students. In many whole-class lessons that consist largely in teacher talk and actions, student self-regulation is at best quite passive and may be directed to other activities (daydreaming, disturbing one's neighbour without being caught, etc.) than to subject-matter learning. However, when students are actively involved in whole-class lessons that entail dialogue with the teacher and with other students about an object of knowledge, it is possible to identify processes of co-regulation conducive to learning. I will briefly mention two examples of studies conducted in primary school classrooms in Geneva. The first example concerns a study of whole-class discussions taking place before a text-writing task in three fifth-grade classes (Allal, Mottier Lopez, Lehraus, & Forget 2005). Our observations showed that the way in which students participated in a series of teacher-led activities, which included brainstorming about text content, elaboration of a writing guide, discussion of what it means to revise a text, had a significant effect on the texts they subsequently produced and on their text revisions. The final texts reflected both the means of regulation constructed collectively (e.g. goals specified in the writing guide) and the students' self-regulation (e.g. students' interpretation of a goal or priority given to a goal when revising his or her text). The second example comes from a year-long study of mathematics problem solving in two third-grade classes (Mottier Lopez & Allal 2007). On the basis of a detailed analysis of whole-class discussions and of students' worksheets, it was possible to trace the ways in which both the teacher and the students contributed to the construction of the 'taken-as-shared meaning' of norms (e.g. what is an 'effective' problem-solving procedure) and the subsequent appropriation of these norms in work carried out by students in small groups or individually. Both of these studies showed that although the teacher's pedagogical and didactical choices about how to organise and direct the lessons are crucial, the actual content produced – expressed orally, written on the blackboard, incorporated in documents – depends to a large extent on the students' contributions. Researchers in didactics use the term 'knowledge text' (*texte du savoir*) to refer to the subject-matter content embodied in what is said and done in the classroom and which constitutes the enacted curriculum of classroom learning. Our findings suggest that the meaning given to subject-matter knowledge results from and, in a cyclical manner, further propels the co-regulation of learning.

What are the implications of the concept of co-regulation and how can it be related to the TLRP principles? I do not see co-regulation as an extra principle to be added on to the TLRP list. Rather I would consider it as an underlying concept that can link together several TLRP principles. In particular, I see it as a way of linking Principle 4: 'Effective pedagogy requires learning to be scaffolded' and Principle 6: 'Effective pedagogy promotes the active engagement of the learner'. The presentation of Principle 4 tends to suggest that scaffolding is something teachers 'provide' to support and regulate learning, rather than something that is constructed through teachers' transactions with learners. In the classical article by Wood, Bruner, and Ross (1976), as in Vygotsky's writings about the zone of proximal development, scaffolding is a process that is elaborated on the basis of what the learner's does and says (given his or her current developmental level) rather than a pre-existing support structure that an expert prepares, introduces and later withdraws. The elaboration of scaffolding cannot take place, in this perspective, without the active engagement of the learner (Principle 6). Active engagement relies on self-regulation that has both metacognitive and motivational dimensions (as described, for example, in the dual-processing model of self-regulation proposed by Boekaerts (1996)). Although enhanced self-regulation can be seen as the end product of scaffolding, in the sense that externally supported forms of regulation are progressively internalised, the learner's initial level of self-regulation is what allows him or her to enter into the activity of scaffolding. In summary, we can consider scaffolding and learner engagement as two interdependent faces of the process of co-regulation of learning.

A concluding perspective

The TLRP principles are designed to orient the actions and decisions of teachers and policy-makers. As such, they specify what teachers and policy-makers can *do* to promote student learning. It would be useful, however, to formulate a second inventory composed of concepts, grounded in theory and in empirical research, that constitute links between the TLRP principles. Co-regulation of learning would be, in my view, one such concept. Other key concepts present in James and Pollard's contribution include: alignment (of teaching, learning, curriculum, assessment), learner and teacher agency, construction of individual and social identities. An enlarged framework for teaching and learning would thus be composed of two dimensions: action-oriented principles and concepts that form conceptual strands linking the principles.

Notes

1. I use the word 'transaction' to include direct face-to-face interactions between students and teachers, as well as more indirect forms of communication (e.g. marks and comments written by teachers on student work) and exchanges mediated by materials in the classroom (e.g. a system of folders students use to file finished work and access new assignments).

2. The two courses with the word 'pedagogy' in the title deal with particular contexts: specialised pedagogy for children with learning difficulties and pedagogies in countries of the southern hemisphere, such as Paulo Freire's 'pedagogy of the oppressed'. The term 'pedagogical' appears in several other course titles (in expressions such as pedagogical practices, pedagogical uses of technology, pedagogical interventions), but this corresponds to a very small fraction of the course offering.

3. Space does not permit examination of the analogous concept of 'co-regulation of teaching', which would refer to the joint influence of teacher self-regulation and of regulation from other sources (students, curriculum materials, professional development activities, educational policies, etc.) on teacher learning as an outcome.

4. The word 'regulation' in English has two meanings: it can refer to an authoritative set of rules to be followed, or to the action of adjusting the functioning of a system on the basis of information provided by the monitoring of its output. The use of 'régulation' in the French psychological and educational literature refers to the second meaning; the word 'règlement' is used for the first meaning. As a consequence, *régulation* has a dynamic connotation in French, whereas in English the idea of imposed 'rules and regulations' is often the first meaning that comes to mind. The literature in English on self-regulated learning is, however, congruent with the French use of the word regulation.

5. An excellent article by Volet, Vauras, and Salonen (2009) reviews several different uses of the term 'co-regulation (or coregulation)'. These authors tend to equate co-regulation with socially mediated forms of regulation and propose a conceptual perspective that integrates self- and co-regulation. In contrast, my use of the term co-regulation refers to the interdependent relations between self- and socially mediated regulation.

References

Alexander, R. 2004. Still no pedagogy? Principle, pragmatism and compliance in primary education *Cambridge Journal of Education* 34, no. 1: 7–34.

Allal, L. 2010. Assessment and the regulation of learning. In *International encyclopedia of education,* Vol. 3, ed. P. Peterson, E. Baker, and B. McGraw, 348–52. Oxford: Elsevier.

Allal, L. 2007. Régulations des apprentissages: Orientations conceptuelles pour la recherché et la pratique en education [Regulation of learning: Conceptual orientations for research and practice in education]. In *Régulation des apprentissages en situation scolaire et en formation [Regulation of learning in school settings and in teacher education].* ed. L. Allal and L. Mottier Lopez, 7–23. Bruxelles: De Boeck.

Allal, L., and L. Mottier Lopez. 2005. Formative assessment of learning: A review of publications in French. In *Formative assessment: Improving learning in secondary classrooms*, ed. J. Looney, 241–64. Paris: OECD.

Allal, L., L. Mottier Lopez, K. Lehraus, and A. Forget. 2005. Whole-class and peer interaction in an activity of writing and revision. In *Writing in context(s): Textual practices and learning processes in sociocultural settings*, ed. T. Kostouli, 69–91. New York: Springer.

Boekaerts, M. 1996. Personality and the psychology of learning. *European Journal of Personality* 10, no. 5: 377–404.

Caillot, M. 2007. The building of a new academic field: The case of French *didactiques*. *European Educational Research Journal* 6, no. 2: 125–30.

Chevallard, Y. 2007. Readjusting didactics to a changing epistemology. *European Educational Research Journal* 6, no. 2: 131–4.

Claparède, E. 1912. *Un institut des sciences de l'éducation et les besoins auxquels il répond [An institute of educational sciences and the needs to which it responds].* Genève: Kündig.

Cobb, P., K. Gravenmeijer, E. Yackel, K. McClain, and J. Whiteneck. 1997. Mathematizing and symbolizing: The emergence of chains of signification in one first-grade classroom. In *Situated cognition: Social, semiotic, and psychological perspectives*, ed. D. Kirshner, and J.A. Whitson, 151–233. Mahwah, NJ: Laurence Erlbaum.

Dolz, J., and B. Schneuwly. 1996. Genres et progression en expression orale et écrite: Éléments de réflexion à propos d'une expérience romande [Genres and progression in oral and written expression: Elements of reflection regarding an experience in French-speaking Switzerland]. *Enjeux* 37–38: 49–75.

Durkheim, E. 1911. Pédagogie [Pedagogy]. In Nouveau dictionnaire de pédagogie et d'instruction primaire [New dictionary of pedagogy and primary instruction], ed. F. Buisson. Paris: Hachette. http://www.inrp.fr/edition-electronique/lodel/dictionnaire-ferdinand-buisson/document.php?id=3355.

Hameline, D. 1998. Pédagogie [Pedagogy]. In *Le pari des sciences de l'éducation, [The educational sciences wager]* ed. R. Hofstetter and B. Schneuwly, 227–41. Bruxelles: De Boeck.

Hofstetter, R. 2010. *Genève: Creuset des sciences de l'éducation* [Geneva: Crucible of educational sciences]. Genève: Droz.

Mottier Lopez, L., and L. Allal. 2007. Sociomathematical norms and the regulation of problem solving in classroom microcultures. *International Journal of Educational Research* 46, no. 5: 252–65.

Piaget, J. 1975. *L'équilibration des structures cognitives: Problème central du développement [Equilibration of cognitive structures: The central problem of development].* Paris: Presses Universitaires de France.

Simon, B. 1981. Why no pedagogy in England? In *Education in the eighties: The central issues*, ed. B. Simon, and W. Taylor, 124–45. London: Batsford.

Wood, D., J.S. Bruner, and G. Ross. 1976. The role of tutoring in problem-solving. *Journal of Child Psychology and Psychiatry* 17, no. 2: 89–100.

Vygotsky, L.S. 1978. *Mind in society: The development of higher psychological processes.* Cambridge, MA: Harvard University Press.

Volet, S., M. Vauras, and P. Salonen. 2009. Self- and social regulation in learning contexts: An integrative perspective. *Educational Psychologist* 44, no. 4: 215–26.

Commonalities and differences: some 'German' observations on TLRP's ten principles for effective pedagogy

Ingrid Gogolin

Faculty of Education, Psychology and Human Movement, University of Hamburg, Germany

The review of TLRP's research that is presented in this volume offers manifold aspects that are worth reflecting on. In my contribution, I concentrate on two aspects that are especially interesting from an international perspective or, more precisely, from a German point of view. The first is a general reflection on the education and science policies that frame educational research in the United Kingdom and Germany. The second is related to the concept of 'effective pedagogy' that is presented in James and Pollard's contribution to this volume. I offer some considerations on research traditions and epistemological frameworks with respect to this concept and illustrate my remarks by looking for commonalities and possible differences between 'effective pedagogy' and the German concepts of 'Bildung' and 'Didaktik'.

Introductory remarks

A major responsibility for academics, we believe, is to look for commonalities.

Mary James and Andrew Pollard, 2011 (in this volume)

There can be no doubt that the TLRP was, and still is, an exceptional endeavour in Europe. From a German point of view, this is, at the same time, both a reason for admiration – if not envy – and some slight disappointment. In my contribution, I will elaborate further on the first aspect; I will do this in the light of the quotation above, taken from James and Pollard's review supporting TLRP's ten principles for effective pedagogy, which is the basis for all contributions to this volume. Their review offers a wealth of aspects that would be worth reflecting on. My selection here is definitely too narrow to do justice to this. From my German point of view, two topics are highly relevant and amenable to comparison – looking for commonalities (and inevitably differences) – between the two contexts.

The first is a general reflection on the education and science policies that frame educational research in both countries. The second is related to the concept of 'effective pedagogy', which is presented by James and Pollard. I will offer some considerations on research traditions and epistemological frameworks with respect to this concept and illustrate my remarks by looking for commonalities between 'effective pedagogy' and the German concepts of 'Bildung' and 'Didaktik'.

In my further contribution, I will not go deeper into the question of what causes my slight disappointment but deal with this only here. The TLRP is – as I said – a huge enterprise, and whatever the outcomes may be in detail, they deserve international attention. I feel very privileged that I came across all this work due to my involvement in international comparative research, to activities in the European Educational Research Association (EERA), and to cooperation with the British Educational Research Association (BERA). Unfortunately though, in a broader German context, hardly any of the research is known; and I would assume that this also applies for, say, France, Spain, Italy, Poland. My guess is that one of the major reasons for this is that there was no deeper interest in publishing outside the English-speaking world. It goes without saying that researchers all over the world, who are interested in international research results, would include English-language publications in their search strategies. But this is unlikely to result in reaping the full harvest of major research initiatives, such as the TLRP, which covers a whole range of topics and specialties manifest in some 100 single projects.

The lack of TLRP publications in relevant books or journals deriving from other European countries (as well as other areas of the world) leads, unfortunately, to a much lower degree of international sharing of knowledge than is desirable. This is all the more regrettable as most editors of books and journals that are based in non-English speaking areas of the world do gladly accept English texts, even if the publication as such would mainly be using the national or local language of the area where the research was based. This remark can be formulated in a different way: as an invitation to all researchers who contributed to TLRP to offer their valuable texts to non-English editors or journals. From a German point of view, it would be worthwhile and rewarding for the advancement of educational research to create a more reciprocal approach to the international sharing of expertise and to knowledge accumulation.

The political framework of educational research

The bold aim of the Teaching and Learning Research Programme (TLRP) was to work to improve outcomes for learners of all ages in teaching and learning contexts across the United Kingdom.

James and Pollard, 2011 (in this volume)

In the last two decades, many European countries have become more and more concerned about the appropriateness and quality of their education systems – for the second time since the 'sputnik shock'. The causes and motives for the occurrence of such doubts, as a major topic of public discourse, differ, as do the starting points of the debates. Undoubtedly, the debate is driven by a political agenda rather than from the inside of the education systems themselves. But the reality of public dissatisfaction with the results of education and schooling is one of the major commonalities that European education systems share (Gogolin, Baumert et al. 2010).

Another commonality seems to be a general distrust of the quality of educational research and its capacity to contribute to the further advancement of education systems. Pollard and James (2010) made the following statement with respect to the British context: 'The origins of TLRP can be traced to the mid-1990s when educational research was heavily criticised for being small scale, irrelevant, inaccessible and low quality' (150). It is easy to identify similar statements with the focus on educational research in other European countries, not least in Germany. Manfred Nießen, Head of the Division Social Sciences and Humanities in the German Research Foundation (DFG), described how educational research was appraised by this research funding organisation, which is, in fact, the most important funding body in Germany: 'In spite of outstanding individual researchers in a variety of sub-disciplines the research base in the universities is too small to provide capacity-building in an internationally competitive way' (Nießen 2010, 162).

This criticism can partly be explained by a growing mistrust in the productivity and performance of research in the social sciences and humanities in general; this is not specific to educational research. A broad disappointment of funders, policy-makers or the general public, with the fact that the determination of research quality in these disciplines evades the strategies that were developed in 'hard science' contexts, seems to be among relevant reasons for this suspicion. These strategies, especially bibliometric methods resulting in citation indices and rankings, are heavily criticised for their methodological weakness and lack of validity, not only from a social sciences and humanities point of view (Bridges 2009; Mocikat 2009; see also http://www.adawis.de/index.php?navigation=1 accessed May 22, 2011). Nevertheless, whilst fully aware of the constraints of these methodologies, the respective instruments, and data deriving from them, are extensively in demand and applied by bodies that conduct processes of research assessment. An excellent example for this is the 2011 Higher Education Funding Council in England (HEFCE) Report on a pilot exercise to develop bibliometric indicators for the Research Excellence Framework: 'The pilot exercise showed that citation information is not sufficiently robust to be used formulaically or as a primary indicator of quality; but there is considerable scope for it to inform and enhance the process of expert review' (http://www.hefce.ac.uk/research/ref/Biblio/ accessed May 22, 2011).

Whereas criticism and distrust are on one side of the coin of appraisal of educational research, and in a more general sense all social sciences and humanities, we find the recognition of their ever-growing societal importance on the other side. An illustration of this is the launching of an online social network on the relevance of social sciences, aiming at the intensification of discourse among researchers, funders, policy-makers and other relevant stakeholders. The launching of this network was commented upon by Ziyad Marar, global publishing director of the publishing house that took the initiative for the development of this network: 'The argument for the importance of social science research and teaching has never been more urgent, and yet the voices making the case are disparate and thus somewhat diffuse in their impact'. (http://sageconnection.wordpress.com/2011/01/12/now-live-major-cross-community-online-network-for-social-science/ accessed May 22, 2011)

In a similar way, the growing importance of educational research has been stated for the German context. In his article, already cited above, Manfred Nießen continued the analysis of the situation:

Somewhat in contrast to this 'frustration', by the end of the 1990s the international large-scale assessment studies – beginning with TIMSS – brought education to the front of public debate. And Erziehungswissenschaft [*educational science*], which by then had acquired a reputation as 'quantité négligeable' in public discourse re-emerged under the label Bildungsforschung [*educational research*] as a respected partner, even setting the agenda to a certain degree. Policy-makers hoped for evidence-based advice and the administration asked for scientifically trained personnel. [*my translations*] (Nießen 2010, 162)

Following the argument presented in James and Pollard (2011, in this volume), this initial situation represents a common argument for an increasing investment in educational research in the last decade, as well as for growing expectations concerning the public benefit of its results.

At this point, however, the commonalities between the initial situation of TLRP, and educational research in Germany, seem to diminish. Whereas the research that is (or was) funded under the umbrella of TLRP focuses on improving educational practice by in-depth analysis *of* this practice, the German development of 'Bildungsforschung' has a clear focus on large-scale surveys that deliver descriptive information about the current situation in the education system at a high level of aggregation. For Germany, the initial impetus for investment in 'Bildungsforschung' derived from the very disappointing results of studies like TIMSS and PISA. The political as well as the general public spheres were alarmed by the discovery that the German educational system – originally a model for public education systems all over the world – did not produce 'top group' student attainment.

The reaction on this discovery was a radical change of research and funding strategies. Whereas, until then, large-scale projects, that included extensive standardised achievement testing, were the exception rather than the rule, such projects were now aggressively promoted and fostered by research funding agencies as well as political funding bodies. Since the results of PISA 2000 were published (Deutsches PISA-Konsortium 2001), a major investment in politically funded research infrastructure has taken place. The following examples may suffice to illustrate this development.

First, the Standing Conference of the Ministers of Education and Cultural Affairs of the Länder in the Federal Republic of Germany – the corporate body that assembles the ministers and senators of the Länder [Federal States] responsible for general education, higher education, research and cultural affairs – founded the Institut zur Qualitätsentwicklung im Bildungswesen (IQB) (Institute for Quality Development of the Education System; see http://www.iqb.hu-berlin.de/institut – accessed May 22, 2011). This institute is now responsible for the operationalisation and standardisation of general aims of education, for the development of tests that allow for the verification of students' attainment, and for a trans-Länder monitoring of the education systems. Secondly, the Standing Conference also commissioned the development of a national report on education since 2006 ('Deutscher Bildungsbericht'). This report presents an empirical review covering the entire German education system. It is published every two years. The report relies on indicator-based information about the system from early childhood education and school education to vocational training, higher education and adult education. It combines statistical parameters that derive from official data and representative research (see http://www.bildungsbericht.de/ – accessed May 22, 2011).

The third example is the National Educational Panel Study (NEPS) (see http://www.uni-bamberg.de/en/neps/ – accessed May 22, 2011) – a major collaborative research initiative that is primarily financed by the Federal Ministry of Education. The general aims of the NEPS are to find out more about educational processes and the impact on individual biographies, and to describe and analyse the major educational trajectories across the lifespan. Roughly 30 research groups were brought together in the interdisciplinary research network, covering a range of disciplines – from educational research, family research, economics and migration studies, to gender and demography studies.

All mentioned developments have a focus on diagnostics, statistics and survey methods in common. The significance of the developments can only be understood in the light of two traditional features of education in Germany.

The first is the usually radically protected cultural sovereignty of the German Länder. This is deeply rooted in the new formation of the German education system after World War II and originally aimed at preventing another abuse of the system by a centralised political regime. In the meantime however, this tradition led to a number of – to say the least – limitations for joint activities and education reforms. One of these is the strict prohibition of the Federal German Government from intervening in the general education system. The only possibility for the Federal Government to legally intervene in the education system is through the funding of research. This explains the focus on research-based activities.

The second traditional feature is a deep distrust of survey methods and standardised testing, which united parents and educational practitioners, as well as policy-makers and researchers over a long period of time in Germany. Until the late 1990s, the demand for standardised testing systems or centralised final exams would have caused a storm of protest. Consequently, the German participation in the TIMSS and PISA studies were at first accompanied by major public questioning and resistance. It was mainly the shocked response to the disastrous PISA results, published in 2001, that lead to a change in public and political opinion. With respect to political decision making, at all levels of the system, the most influential educational researchers in Germany, at the time, were or are involved in the TIMSS and PISA studies. All leading positions within the newly invented structures, mentioned above, are held by researchers from the respective research consortia.

This development sets the frame for drawing a clear distinction between TLRP's and the current German mainstream understanding of 'evidence' for 'effectiveness' deriving from educational research. Whereas the TLRP emphasises a notion of 'evidence information' that can justify the formulation of principles for innovation in pedagogy *without* being based on measures of direct impact on leaner outcomes, the current German mainstream – most politically influential educational researchers as well as policy-makers – concentrates mainly on measurement, monitoring and control. The service the education system provides for economic productivity, and personal development as functionality associated with this, are the focus of attention. This is accompanied by the introduction of new governance strategies that derive from economic practice applied to social systems in general, and especially to the entire educational system. The effectiveness of these governance strategies has to be controlled and can be controlled via the application of identical, or at least similar, instruments to those being developed and implemented for the purpose of assessing the educational effectiveness of the system.

In order to give an example of the described difference between research strategies that were promoted by TLRP, and actual preferences in Germany, I refer to TLRP's clear commitment to research in authentic educational settings. Whereas insight in authentic settings was a generally accepted and widely practised educational research strategy in Germany until the late 1990s, it is today severely questioned by the above mentioned influential research groups who are ardent proponents of experimental designs. To them, research carried out in authentic educational settings is unable to contribute to any notion of 'evidence' because it does not fulfil the requirement of interventions being tested against a control group without treatment. Both positions – the relevance of authentic settings for the possibility of gaining insight into the 'multilayered nature of innovation in pedagogy' (James and Pollard 2011, in this volume) and the denial of the possibility for such research to render 'unequivocal evidence' – are subjects of disputation in the German educational research community (Prenzel, Gogolin et al. 2008). Fortunately, this dispute is still going on – and the TLRP position as presented in the 'Ten principles for effective pedagogy' will contribute constructively to it.

'Effective pedagogy'

TLRP's *commitment to work 'to improve outcomes for learners' implied a belief that educational progress is possible.*

James and Pollard, 2011 (in this volume)

It is most interesting, from a German point of view, that deliberations about appropriate conclusions to be drawn from TLRP's work have led to the claim that the programme contributed to the advancement of pedagogy rather than of 'teaching and learning'. With reference to Brian Simon (1981), James and Pollard state that the term pedagogy refers to the multidisciplinary and scientific tradition of educational thought and practice in Europe, whereas the notion of 'teaching and learning' refers to a more instrumental approach that can be found in the British context.

The definition of 'effective pedagogy' as offered by James and Pollard, with reference to Simon, starts from what children have in common as members of the human species, establishes general principles of teaching, and determines the modifications of practice that are necessary to meet specific individual needs. This is very interesting from a German (or, more generally, a central European) point of view, because allusions to the concepts of 'Bildung' and 'Didaktik' can be heard therein. A broader discourse on the different European conceptual approaches to teaching, learning, instruction, 'Bildung' and didactics is just being started by a European network of educational researchers who meet through the agency of the European Educational Research Association (EERA). The first publication deriving from their comparative work assembles the 'common ground' that can be discovered when going beyond the fragmentations and differences that become visible on the surface of national or local traditions in educational theory and practice (Hudson and Meyer 2011).

A relevant discourse in this context, which also refers to a longer lasting theoretical debate among German educational researchers, concerns the perspective that is taken with respect to the learner in teaching and learning. The traditional notions of 'Bildung' – as the underlying theory – and 'Didaktik' – as the operative strategy – derived from a normative perspective. This posed the question: what is it that the members of the human species have in common, and, thus, sets the frame for the categorical aims of education? Answers to the question of how children are to be guided on their way to achieve the ultimate aims in their process of 'Bildung', that were given within the framework of 'Didaktik', derived from normatively driven theoretical assumptions that also relate to considerations about children's modes and capacities to learn. The golden thread of didactical constructions in this tradition was built by suppositions about the best ways to teach. Learning, in this perspective, was seen as a function of teaching, less so as an activity of a learner. Indeed, there was hardly any empirical research on the connectivity between the strategies of teaching and the learning strategies of children.

This tradition became criticised not least in the context of educational research on the consequences of migration for education (Gogolin and Nauck 2000; Koller 2002). In this framework, the research focus was shifted, from emphasis on the assumption that education addresses the 'average normal' child, to a perspective that takes into account the individual predispositions for learning, which influence the processes of accepting and adapting to the 'offers' made by teaching. In the related discourse, the British tradition of emphasising the individual child was intensely discussed – and highly appreciated.

The development of TLRP's ten principles, as described by James and Pollard, 'beginning with pedagogical aims, and the way these are expressed in classroom practice, and extending to the conditions needed for effective pedagogy in the structures and cultures of schooling and the wider environment, including social and educational policy, locally and nationally' (277, in this volume), holds a moment of surprise in the light of this experience from the German context. The learner seems to be absent here. However, in some of the principles, namely, Principle 3 *Effective pedagogy recognises the importance of prior experience and learning*', the learner appears as an actor in the process. Moreover, some of the TLRP projects presented by James and Pollard in order to illustrate Principles 6, 7 and 8 relate to the learners' perspective, and it is stated that, '[...] in an era which saw a steady growth, within much of the UK, of central control over curriculum, pedagogy and assessment, the engagement of learners has become an increasingly pressing contemporary issue' (297, in this volume).

To me, the relation between a pedagogy, which takes a starting point from 'what children have in common as members of the human species', and an approach to 'Bildung', which takes the learner as an actor into account, is worthy of further discussion and exploration. This is only one example that supports the value of presenting TLRP's ten principles to a broader European public. It will hopefully initiate, as it did in the British context, a broader evidence-informed international discourse that, no doubt, will contribute to the progressive development of global understanding of effective teaching and learning.

References

Bridges, D. 2009. Research quality assessment: Impossible science, possible art? *British Educational Research Journal* 35, no. 4: 497–517.

Deutsches PISA-Konsortium, ed. 2001. *PISA 2000. Basiskompetenzen von Schülerinnen und Schülern im internationalen Vergleich*. Opladen: Leske+Budrich.

Gogolin, I., Baumert, et al., eds. 2010. *Transforming education. Umbau des Bildungswesens. Large-scale reform projects and their effects. Bildungspolitische Großreformprojekte und ihre Effekte Beiheft 13*. Wiesbaden: ZfE VS-Verlag.

Gogolin, I., and B. Nauck, eds. 2000. *Migration, gesellschaftliche Differenzierung und Bildung. Resultate des Forschungsschwerpunktprogramms FABER*. Opladen: Leske+Budrich.

Hudson, B., and M.A. Meyer, eds. 2011. *Beyond fragmentation: Didactics learning and teaching in Europe*. Opladen: Barbara Budrich.

Koller, H-C. 2002. Bildung und Migration. Bildungstheoretische Überlegungen im Anschluss an Bourdieu und Cultural Studies. In *Bildung/Transformation. Kulturelle und gesellschaftliche Umbrüche aus bildungstheoretischer Perspektive*, ed. W. Friedrichs and O. Sanders, 181–200. Bielefeld: Transcript.

Mocikat, R. 2009. Arbeitskreis Deutsch als Wissenschaftssprache (ADAWIS) Interview. *Forschung* 3–4: 112–4.

Nießen, M. 2010. Building structures by research funding? DFG's programme in the field of empirical research in education. In *Transforming education. Umbau des Bildungswesens. Large-scale reform projects and their effects. Bildungspolitische Großreformprojekte und ihre Effekte*, ed. I. Gogolin, J. Baumert, and A. Scheunpflug. Wiesbaden: ZfE VS-Verlag. Beiheft 13.

Pollard, A., and M. James. 2010. The UK's teaching and learning research programme (TLRP): Strategies and contributions to large-scale reform. In *Transforming education. Umbau des Bildungswesens. Large-scale reform projects and their effects Bildungspolitische Großreformprojekte und ihre Effekte*, ed. I. Gogolin, J. Baumert, and A. Scheunpflug. Wiesbaden: ZfE VS-Verlag. Beiheft 13.

Prenzel, M., I. Gogolin, et al., eds. 2008. Kompetenzdiagnostik. Zeitschrift für Erziehungswissenschaft. Sonderheft. 08/2007. Wiesbaden: VS Verlag.

Simon, B. 1981. Why no pedagogy in England? In *Education in the eighties: The central issues*, ed. B. Simon and W. Taylor. London: Batsford.

Contributions to innovative learning and teaching? Effective research-based pedagogy – a response to TLRP's principles from a European perspective[1]

Filip Dochy, Inneke Berghmans, Eva Kyndt and Marlies Baeten

Centre for Research on Professional Learning, Development, Corporate Training and Lifelong Learning, University of Leuven, Belgium

Starting from the contribution on the 'ten principles of effective pedagogy' by James and Pollard, we critically reflect on some of the principles and assess whether these principles can be grounded in the wider European research literature that has accumulated internationally. We conclude that these principles can be supported and expressed in the following statements. First, prior knowledge and experience is a springboard for future learning. Secondly, taking students' perceptions into account is crucial when providing activities and structures of intellectual, social and emotional support for learning. Thirdly, autonomous motivation and appropriate workload are essential as driving forces for engagement. Fourthly, engagement is a driving force in establishing a lifelong learning habit. Fifthly, student-centred teaching methods should provide direct instructional guidance to safeguard engagement. Sixthly, striving towards cooperative learning environments and team learning requires psychological safety and group interdependence to establish mutually shared cognition in groups. Seventhly, informal learning and learning climate influence retention of learning by professionals; professionals seems to develop 'learning patterns', and students should be prepared with this in mind. And finally, those who support the learning of others should learn continuously, supported themselves through practice-based inquiry. These statements are underpinned with recent research in this contribution.

Introduction

There is no doubt that the 'ten principles of effective pedagogy' presented, as a result of the TLRP programme, are well thought through and research based. Nevertheless, they might be received by practitioners as common sense and perhaps 'too broad'. Using the contribution on the 'ten principles of effective pedagogy' by James and Pollard (2011, in this volume), we will critically reflect on some of the principles, and assess whether these principles can be grounded in the wider literature that has accumulated internationally. Of course, in our current contribution, the view we present will be taken from a team perspective that is biased by the research we have been involved in over the past decade, much of which has been based in settings other than in schools. However, since TLRP developed its principles to apply across the life course, our reflections are relevant. Certainly, our research is influenced strongly by many other European researchers because we share our results and concerns on many occasions such as European Association for Research on Learning and Instruction (EARLI) and European Association of Work and Organizational Psychology (EAWOP) conferences.

Prior knowledge and experience is a springboard for future learning

Vygotsky and others stressed the importance of prior learning and experience as a basis of effective pedagogy (TLRP Principle 3). Nowadays, this statement seems so strong that the advice seems to be that any practitioner should take it into account, and any researcher should include prior learning as a variable. At the turn of the twenty-first century, we published a review of research (Dochy, Segers, and Buehl 1999) related to the effects of the use of prior knowledge on performance. We described these effects from the perspective of the assessment methods used to assess the dependent variable 'prior knowledge'. The review revealed that a vast majority of studies report direct, positive effects of prior knowledge. The small number of studies showing negative or no effects of prior knowledge on performance used particularly flawed assessment methods. More recently, Hailikari and others have investigated the influence of prior knowledge in mathematics, pharmacy and sciences and confirmed these results (Hailikari, Nevgi, and Lindblom-Ylänne 2007; Hailikari, Katajavuori, and Lindblom-Ylänne 2008; Hailikari and Nevgi 2010).

Taking students' perceptions into account is crucial when providing activities and structures of intellectual, social and emotional support for learning

The importance of taking students' perceptions into account strongly relates to TLRP's fourth principle of effective pedagogy. In this respect, research by Berghmans, Dochy, and Struyven (submitted) found that scaffolding is not always widely appreciated by students. Instead, their study revealed that students were significantly less satisfied with a tutor that questions and challenges them. They tend to be more satisfied with a directive tutor who informs them, gives specific answers to their questions and demonstrates course content. Diverse concerns related to the constructivist-oriented facilitative approach were reported, i.e. lack of structure and clarity, lack of modelling and lack of immediate feedback (Berghmans, Dochy, and Struyven submitted). Constructivism leads us to striving for 'collective, reciprocal, supportive, cumulative and purposeful teacher-student dialogue' (James and Pollard 2011 in this volume). In order to achieve this, we agree with Alexander (2001, 2006) that teachers and students should build on their own and each other's ideas, and, as such, make coherent lines of thinking and enquiry. However, our research (Berghmans, Dochy, and Struyven submitted) shows that not all students are open to constructivist types of learning and teaching talk as described by Alexander (2001, 2006). More specifically, some students prefer getting information and answers directly from their tutors since questioning and prompting, which generates a forum for discussion, is perceived as confusing and lacking overview and clarity. This attitude can, however, also be explained by what students are used to since not every student (or educational institution) is that familiar with constructivist-oriented scaffolding styles (Berghmans, Dochy, and Struyven submitted). As such, in order for principles of effective pedagogy to be truly effective, they need to be acknowledged and implemented at all levels of education, gradually preparing learners to handle expectations and responsibilities related to these principles. As a discrepancy seems to exist between constructivist practices supported by the research evidence, and students' preferences and experiences with these practices, students' perceptions and experiences should be taken into account when applying the principles of effective pedagogy. As a consequence, alignment in all levels of education and preparing students is even more essential.

Furthermore, it is not necessarily the learning environment in itself that influences learning, but the way students perceive the learning environment. As such, we found that learning environments that were perceived most positively had most beneficial outcomes in terms of students' learning (Baeten, Dochy, and Struyven 2011; Nijhuis, Segers, and Gijselaers 2005; Struyven et al. 2006, 2008). Nijhuis, Segers, and Gijselaers (2005) found that students perceived a problem-based learning course as less positive compared with an assignment-based learning course. In addition, surface learning increased and deep learning decreased in the problem-based learning course, compared with the assignment-based learning course. In line with these findings, Struyven et al. (2006, 2008) found that students' perceptions of student-activating settings were significantly less positive than perceptions of lecture-based settings, and accordingly, students adopted more surface approaches in the student-activating settings. Finally, Baeten and Dochy (2011) found that a gradually implemented case-based learning environment, which was most beneficial for students' approaches to learning, was also perceived most positively. Thus, it can be concluded that when students' perceptions are positive or negative, their learning may be respectively enhanced or put at risk (Struyven et al. 2008).

Autonomous motivation and appropriate workload are essential as driving forces for engagement

TLRP Principle 6 highlights the importance of developing active engagement, positive learning dispositions, self-confidence and learning awareness. It is stated that the promotion of learner independence and autonomy results in more effective learning, and it also contributes to personal development (formation). First, we can confirm from our own research that motivation and autonomy play an import role in the learning of students. We found that when students are autonomously motivated, they are more inclined to apply deep approaches to learning (Kyndt et al. 2011). These deep approaches to learning reflect an intention to comprehend the material, to use strategies such as critical thinking, using various sources and relating ideas (Biggs 2001). However, which specific strategies are the best to accomplish active conceptual analysis depends on the task in hand (Entwistle, McCune, and Walker 2001). Prior research has shown that workload is a discouraging factor for the adoption of a deep approach to learning (Baeten et al. 2010). The importance of autonomous motivation for the development of students also comes to the fore in the finding that autonomously motivated students keep applying more deep approaches than their fellow students when workload is high (Kyndt et al. 2011; Kyndt et al. submitted). Autonomously motivated students seem to cope better with workload than other students.

Engagement is a driving force in establishing a lifelong learning habit

The research study of Brooks and Everett (2008) showed that the independence that students experience within higher education affects their future learning. Higher education graduates indicated that their lifelong learning process was mostly influenced by the fact that they had to study independently in higher education. They reported that independent study gave them the necessary skills and motivation to engage in future learning through formal and informal routes. Social changes, such as globalisation, international economic interdependences, economic competitiveness and the increasing importance of knowledge have led to the awareness that both individuals and organisations need to engage in lifelong learning (Baert 2002; Pillay, Boulton-Lewis, and Wilss 2003; Beck and Achtenhagen 2007). Lifelong learning is understood as a process, in which both individuals and organisations, in all contexts of their functioning, acquire the needed knowledge and competences to be able to realise all their professional, economic, social and cultural responsibilities in a rapid changing society and to be able to adopt a critical, meaning giving and responsible attitude (Baert 2002). Although research has shown that the initial level of education obtained by an individual is an important predictor for participation in lifelong learning (Brooks and Everett 2008; Fitzgerald, Taylor, and LaValle 2003; Kyndt et al. 2011), higher education has been criticised for not developing competences, such as critical thinking, self management and the ability to solve novel and complex problems, which are needed for professional expertise in this society (Boyatzis, Stubbs, and Taylor 2002; Kember et al. 1997; Neilsen 2000; Segers, Nijhuis, and Gijselaers 2006; Tynjälä 1999).

By implementing student-centred learning environments – characterised by activity and independence of the student, with the teacher in a responsive coaching role, and knowledge as a tool instead of an aim (Dochy et al. 2002) – higher education hopes to equip its students with the necessary competences for their future lifespan.

Student-centred teaching methods should provide direct instructional guidance to safeguard engagement

The development of student-centred teaching methods, such as problem-based and case-based learning, is in line with the TLRP's Principle 6 stating that effective pedagogy should promote the active engagement of the learner. The origin of these teaching methods goes back to constructivist learning theory, which states that learning is an 'active process in which learners are active sense makers who seek to build coherent and organised knowledge' (Mayer 2004, 14). It has been widely expected that student-centred teaching methods improve educational outcomes in higher education (e.g. Lea, Stephenson, and Troy 2003). However, reviews of studies comparing the effectiveness of student-centred teaching versus conventional, i.e. mainly lecture-based, teaching show limited evidence of the benefits of student-centred approaches for educational outcomes.

The review studies of Colliver (2000) and Smits et al. (2003) found no persuasive evidence that problem-based learning enhanced students' knowledge and performance. However, Albanese and Mitchell (1993) and Vernon and Blake (1993) made a distinction between knowledge and clinical performance and found that medical students in problem-based learning scored better on clinical performance, compared with conventionally taught students, but they scored lower or at the same level on basic knowledge. Similarly, our own review study (Dochy et al. 2003) showed that students in problem-based learning settings scored better on skills (i.e. the application of knowledge), but not necessarily on knowledge acquisition. Kirschner, Sweller, and Clark (2006) explain the scores on knowledge acquisition by stating that discovery learning makes heavy demands on working memory, since it is used to process and retrieve information. Consequently, working memory is not available and cannot contribute to the accumulation of knowledge in long-term memory. Therefore, Kirschner, Sweller, and Clark (2006) suggest that students, and in particular novice students, should be provided with direct instructional guidance (e.g. providing students with information that explains the course contents) since they lack appropriate schemas to integrate new information with prior knowledge.

We are not only interested in quantitative learning outcomes but also in the quality of the learning process. Therefore, we conducted a review study that investigated the effects of student-centred teaching methods on students' approaches to learning, without focusing on one teaching method in particular (Baeten et al. 2010). This review study did not find consistent results. Whereas some empirical studies emphasised the added value of student-centred teaching for fostering deep approaches, other empirical studies found the opposite, i.e. more surface approaches in student-centred learning environments. The latter finding was also supported by our own study (Struyven et al. 2006), in which we compared student-activating teaching and lectures.

Research suggests that active engagement is not necessarily always beneficial for students' learning. Instead, it emphasises the importance of direct instructional guidance in student-centred settings, for instance by implementing lectures or a directive tutoring approach. Direct instructional guidance may help students to become familiar with the discipline, basic concepts and outline of the course (Albanese and Mitchell 1993). However, when there is a gradual transition towards a learning environment that makes strong appeal to students' responsibility in learning, students can adjust their learning style and role to the student-centred approach (Choi, Lee, and Kang 2009; Hung 2009). As such, appropriate scaffolding is indeed of utmost importance. We investigated the effects of lecture-based and student-centred teaching (i.e. case-based learning), implemented either solely or in combination (i.e. an alternation of lectures and case-based learning or as a gradual implementation of case-based learning). Our results showed that students benefitted the most when case-based learning was introduced gradually, so that there was an incremental transition from lecture-based to case-based learning. Students in this setting scored the highest on monitoring studying, organised studying and effort management, and the lowest on surface approach (Baeten et al. 2011).

Striving towards cooperative learning environments and team learning requires psychological safety and group interdependence to establish mutually shared cognition in groups

In addition to TLRP's sixth principle of active involvement, more attention should be paid to cooperative learning environments and team learning, as advocated in TLRP Principle 7. A diverse spectrum of methodologies has been introduced, the hallmarks of which are that learners work together and create knowledge throughout interactive discourse, i.e. collaborative learning, cooperative learning, team learning and peer-assisted learning (Kyndt et al. 2011; Parr and Townsend 2002). Literature has been dominated by studies that claim diverse effects of these 'interactive' methodologies on academic achievement, approaches to learning, affective and social outcomes (e.g. Johnson and Johnson 2000; Topping 1996). Based on these studies, it is clear that research supports the seventh principle of effective pedagogy. In order to understand the aforementioned effects in depth, more attention should be given to the underlying processes and dynamics occurring in these learning environments, which James and Pollard (2011, in this volume) also acknowledge in their review of TLRP project work. Recent research has aimed to shed more light on what makes team learning successful in schools and in organisational contexts. Effective team learning requires the establishment of a dialogical space in which 'sharing', 'co-construction' and 'constructive conflict' are crucial (Decuyper, Dochy, and Van den Bossche 2010). Sharing (or construction) refers to articulating one's personal meaning. This can evolve into co-construction as sharing leads to a process of negotiation and mutually building meaning, which refines, develops or modifies the original meaning. Finally, constructive conflict refers to an elaborated discussion, inviting divergence, dissent and open communication that leads to further communication and some kind of temporary agreement (Decuyper, Dochy, and Van den Bossche 2010).

Recent research on team learning has crossed boundaries (of educational sciences, labour pedagogy, organisational psychology, business studies and management studies) and accumulated knowledge from different disciplines studying similar phenomena, such as cooperative learning and team learning. The research on teams conducted in many different settings, such as student teams, work teams, business teams, volleyball teams, other sports teams, police and firemen teams and military teams, consistently shows that group interdependence and psychological safety are the two most important group characteristics to influence learning in teams (Decuyper, Dochy, and Van den Bossche 2010; Dochy, Kyndt, and Veestraeten submitted). While positive group interdependence refers to cooperation, negative group interdependence concerns competition. In general, positive interdependence tends to result in higher outcome levels compared with negative or no interdependence among team members (Decuyper, Dochy, and Van den Bossche 2010). Furthermore, the degree to which group members feel psychologically safe or have 'a sense of confidence that the team will not embarrass, reject, or punish someone for speaking up' (Edmondson 1999, 354), has a significant, and mostly the largest, predictive value on the effectiveness of the group (Decuyper, Dochy, and Van den Bossche 2010; Dochy, Kyndt, and Veestraeten submitted). A lack of psychological safety is reported to inhibit important team learning behaviours such as experimenting and seeking help. In contrast, psychological safety creates opportunities to engage in team learning behaviour that asks team members to build on and to disagree with one another (Van den Bossche et al. 2006).

Recent research combines two dominant perspectives on collaborative work and learning – the social and the cognitive perspective – since both social processes, as well as (socio-) cognitive processes and outcomes, are important in learning in groups. While the social perspective stresses the influence of social factors on successful team performance, the cognitive perspective traditionally investigates how information processing takes place within the individual, how individuals assess and interpret different situations and how they solve complex problems. During social, collective collaboration in teams, these individual cognitions and knowledge structures become integrated and coordinated at the inter-individual level. Research suggests that such team cognitive structures – or shared mental models – facilitate coordination and communication in the performance of teams. As team members interact with one another and are constantly engaged in dynamic and interdependent processes, the social and socio-cognitive processes on the level of the team need to be taken into consideration when studying team performance (Barron 2003; Van den Bossche et al. 2006).

Team learning or group-level learning is an emergent property of the group and is distinguished from individual learning within the context of a group (Wilson, Goodman, and Cronin 2007). This means that team members can learn and their learning can improve the team's performance, but it remains individual learning unless it is shared by the team members: 'If an individual leaves the group and the group cannot access his or her learning, the group has failed to learn' (Wilson, Goodman, and Cronin 2007, 1042). The research of De Dreu (2007), in which the effect of the interaction between cooperative outcome interdependence and task reflexivity on team effectiveness is mediated by learning, can be considered as evidence for the relationship between team learning and team effectiveness. Our own research (Decuyper, Dochy, and Van den Bossche 2010) showed that team learning behaviour (construction, co-construction and constructive conflict) is a predictor for mutually shared cognition and team effectiveness. Moreover, team learning behaviour and shared mental models do influence team effectiveness.

Building on our research, as well as on earlier studies, one has to conclude that an awareness and thorough consideration of these processes are crucial for TLRP's Principle 7 to be a true indicator of 'effective' pedagogy.

Informal learning and learning climate influence retention of learning by professionals; professionals seem to develop 'learning patterns'; students should be prepared with this in mind

TLRP Principle 8 asserts the significance of informal learning and that it should be utilised in formal settings. This principle is in line with the thought that formal and informal learning should be understood as complementary (Cofer 2000). James and Pollard (2011, in this volume) write: 'the TLRP Directors' Team was committed to exploring whether they (the ten principles) might apply elsewhere (outside of school projects)'. Research on (the importance of) informal learning has also been focusing on professional learning within organisations. It was found that employees value the fact that they can keep on learning and developing within their jobs. When they experience a positive learning climate within their organisation, they are more inclined to remain working for that organisation (Govaerts et al. 2011; Kyndt et al. 2009b). In addition, an organisation can facilitate informal learning by means of culture, policy and specific procedures (Marsick and Watkins 1990). In our research, we investigated the presence of learning conditions within organisations (Kyndt, Dochy, and Nijs 2009a). One of the learning conditions that was identified in this research, which we would like to highlight, in line with the TLRP's work on technology, is the presence and availability of modern communication tools and technology. The study showed that the availability of communication tools and technologies within organisations has the potential to stimulate informal learning (Kyndt, Dochy, and Nijs 2009a). We refer to it as having potential because 'while the organisation of work sets the context and conditions for learning, it is still the reciprocal interaction between the individual and the workplace that determines learning' (Tynjälä 2008, 12). To our knowledge, current research has not yet proven that this is more than 'a potential'; research in this area is still scarce. The research of Govaerts and Baert (submitted) investigated whether different configurations of formal learning activities and informal learning conditions were present in different organisations. These researchers concluded that different organisations have different configurations or 'learning patterns'. Future research will investigate whether different learning patterns can be related to different (organisational) goals.

Those who support the learning of others should learn continuously, supported through practice-based inquiry

Finally, in order to critically assess or implement the learning environments described above, instructional approaches, or principles for effective pedagogy, priority needs to be given to the professional learning of the educator. Supporting the TLRP's Principle 9 of effective pedagogy, we affirm that a need exists for educators to continuously learn with and from one another in order to cope with increasing demands of contemporary and future educational practice. In our research, it was found that peer learning occurs mostly informally and spontaneously instead of formally through organised events (Govaerts et al. 2010). More specifically, peer mentoring and peer coaching have proved to be valuable peer learning methodologies. Peer mentoring can be defined as an intentional one-on-one reciprocal relationship between employees at a same or similar lateral level in the organisation, which is characterised by a degree of mutuality that enables both individuals to experience being mentor and mentee (Eby 1997; Parker, Hall, and Kram 2008). Both new and experienced professionals can benefit from this learning partnership as know-how and expertise are shared, discussed, renewed and validated (Eisen 2001a; Eisen 2001b). More specifically, peer mentoring serves different functions within the educational field, for example, coaching and learning facilitation, personal and emotional support, career development, role modelling, strategies and systems advice, and, finally, advocacy. However, it seems that not every function is that common in every level of education. For instance, teachers from primary schools scored significantly higher on the function of personal and emotional support than teachers from secondary schools and teachers from institutions of higher education (Ieven et al. 2010).

Educational institutions and organisations should invest in formal and informal learning opportunities through which professional development can occur. In recent years, initiatives at the international level have been taken in order to support such professional development. Examples are the rise of more practice-oriented journals (such as *Practical Research and Assessment* and the *Canadian Journal of Practice-based Research in Theatre*) and the founding of associations that support such development (such as the European Association for Practitioner Research on Improving Learning in Education and the Professions, EAPRIL). Sharing knowledge and experiences and results of practice enquiry is the main goal and stimulates professionals from all over Europe to develop themselves through interaction. Group interdependence and psychological safety, mentioned above, are also in this context vital to stimulate successful learning. These practices of challenging one's assumptions, sharing information and boundary crossing activities are, however, sometimes considered threatening by many scholars (e.g. James and Pollard 2011, in this volume; Washer 2006). We believe that the key to openness to these learning experiences may lie in the ultimate goal for which every educator strives – that is, to improve students' learning in order for our learners to become highly self-efficacious and self-regulating individuals who can obtain and secure their own significant place at the workplace and, in general, in the society. TLRP's principles of effective pedagogy seem to be a good guide when striving for this goal.

Acknowledgments

The contribution of Marlies Baeten is supported by an Aspirant FWO grant of the Fund for Scientific Research Flanders (FWO Vlaanderen).

Note

1. This article is dedicated to Professor Dr Emeritus H. Baert, University of Leuven, Belgium.

References

Albanese, M., and S. Mitchell. 1993. Problem-based learning: A review of the literature on its outcome and implementation issues. *Academic Medicine* 68: 52–81.

Alexander, R. 2001. *Culture and pedagogy: International comparisons in primary education.* Oxford: Blackwell.

Alexander, R. 2006. *Education as dialogue. Moral and pedagogical choices for a runaway world.* Hong Kong: HKIED in conjunction with Dialogos UK.

Baert, H. 2002. Spanningsvelden in het discours van de officiële verklaringen over levenslang leren [Tensions in discourses on official statements about lifelong learning]. In *Levenslang leren en de actieve welvaartstaat [Lifelong learning and the active welfare state].* ed. H. Baert, L. Dekeyser and G. Sterck. 17–34. Leuven: Acco.

Baeten, M., F. Dochy, and K. Struyven. 2011. *Enhancing students' approaches to learning: The added value of gradually implementing case-based learning.* Paper to be presented at the 14th Biennial Conference of the European Association for Research on Learning and Instruction, August, in Exeter, United Kingdom.

Baeten, M., E. Kyndt, K. Struyven, and F. Dochy. 2010. Using student-centred learning environments to stimulate deep approaches to learning: Factors encouraging or discouraging their effectiveness. *Educational Research Review* 5, no. 3: 243–60.

Barron, B. 2003. When smart groups fail. *The Journal of the Learning Sciences* 12: 307–59.

Beck, K., and F. Achterhagen. 2007. *Vocational education and training in a globalized world*. Göttingen: Georg-August-Universität Göttingen.

Berghmans, I., F. Dochy, and K. Struyven. (2011, submitted). The effects of approaches to tutoring on students' learning in higher education. *Instructional Science*.

Biggs, J. 2001. Enhancing learning: A matter of style or approach? In *Perspectives on thinking, learning, and cognitive styles*, ed. R.J. Sternberg and L. Zhang, 73–102. Mahwah, NJ: Erlbaum.

Boyatzis, R.E., E.C. Stubbs, and S.N. Taylor. 2002. Learning cognitive and emotional intelligence competences through graduate management education. *Academy of Management Journal on Learning and Education* 1, no. 2: 150–62.

Brooks, R., and G. Everett. 2008. The impact of higher education on lifelong learning. *International Journal of Lifelong Education* 27, no. 3: 239–54.

Choi, I., S. Lee, and J. Kang. 2009. Implementing a case-based e-learning environment in a lecture-oriented anaesthesiology class: Do learning styles matter in complex problem solving over time? *British Journal of Educational Technology* 40, no. 5: 933–47.

Cofer, D.A. 2000. *Informal workplace learning: Practice application brief no. 10*. Columbus, OH: ERIC Clearinghouse on Adult, Career, and Vocational Education. http://www.calpro-online.org/ERIC/docs/pab00019.pdf. (accessed March 16, 2011).

Colliver, J. 2000. Effectiveness of problem-based learning curricula: Research and theory. *Academic Medicine* 75, no. 3: 259–66.

Decuyper, S., F. Dochy, and P. Van den Bossche. 2010. Grasping the dynamic complexity of team learning: An integrative model for effective team learning in organisations. *Educational Research Review* 5, no. 2: 111–33.

De Dreu, C.K.W. 2007. Cooperative outcome interdependence, task reflexivity and team effectiveness: A motivated information processing approach. *Journal of Applied Psychology* 92: 628–38.

Dochy, F., E. Kyndt, and M. Veestraeten. (2011, submitted). The effect of social and cognitive factors on team learning and team effectiveness in military teams. *Small Group Research*.

Dochy, F., M. Segers, and M. Buehl. 1999. The relation between assessment practices and outcomes of studies: The case of research on prior knowledge. *Review of Educational Research* 69, no. 2: 145–86.

Dochy, F., M. Segers, D. Gijbels, and P. Van den Bossche. 2002. *Studentgericht onderwijs and probleemgestuurd onderwijs. Betekenis, achtergronden en effecten*. Utrecht: Lemma.

Dochy, F., M. Segers, P. Van den Bossche, and D. Gijbels. 2003. Effects of problem-based learning: A meta-analysis. *Learning and Instruction* 13: 533–68.

Eby, L. 1997. Alternative forms of mentoring in changing organizational environments: A conceptual extension of the mentoring literature. *Journal of Vocational Behaviour* 51: 125–44.

Edmondson, A.C. 1999. Psychological safety and learning behaviour in work teams. *Administrative Science Quarterly* 44, no. 2: 350–83.

Eisen, M.-J. 2001a. Peer-based professional development viewed through the lens of transformative learning. *Holistic Nursing Practice* 16, no. 1: 30–42.

Eisen, M.-J. 2001b. Peer-based learning: A new-old alternative to professional development. *Adult Learning* 12, no. 1: 9–10.

Entwistle, N., V. McCune, and P. Walker. 2001. Conceptions, styles, and approaches within higher education: Analytical abstractions and everyday experience. In *Perspectives on cognitive, learning and thinking styles*, ed. R.J. Sternberg and L.-F. Zhang, 103–36. Mahwah, NJ: Erlbaum.

Fitzgerald, R., R. Taylor, and I. LaValle. 2003. *National adult learning survey 2002* [Research report 415]. London, UK: Department for Education and Skills.

Govaerts, N., and H. Baert. (submitted). Learning patterns in organisations: Towards a typology of workplace-learning configurations. *Human Resource Development International*.

Govaerts, N., E. Kyndt, F. Dochy, and H. Baert. 2011. The influence of learning and working climate on the retention of talented employees. *Journal of Workplace Learning* 23, no. 1: 35–55.

Govaerts, N., C. Kinschots, F. Dochy, and I. Berghmans. 2010. Vormen en functies *van Peer Learning in organisaties en de relatie met retentie van werknemers* [Types and functions of Peer Learning in organisations and their relationship with employee's retention]. Unpublished master's thesis, Catholic University of Leuven, Belgium.

Hailikari, T., A. Nevgi, and S. Lindblom-Ylänne. 2007. Exploring alternative ways of assessing prior knowledge, its components and their relation to learning outcome. A mathematics-based case study. *Studies in Educational Evaluation* 33: 320–37.

Hailikari, T., N. Katajavuori, and S. Lindblom-Ylänne. 2008. Prior knowledge and its relevance in learning and instructional design. *American Journal of Pharmaceutical Education* 72, no. 5: 1–9.

Hailikari, T., and A. Nevgi. 2010. How to diagnose at-risk students in chemistry. The case of prior knowledge assessment. *International Journal of Science Education* 32, no. 15: 2079–95.

Hung, W. 2009. The 9-step problem design process for problem-based learning: Application of the 3C3R model. *Educational Research Review* 4: 118–41.

Ieven, I., C. Kinschots, F. Dochy, and I. Berghmans. 2010. *Workplace learning and Peer Mentoring.* Unpublished master's thesis, Catholic University of Leuven, Belgium.

Johnson, D.W., and F. Johnson. 2000. *Joining together: Group theory and group skills.* 7th ed. Boston: Allyn & Bacon.

Kember, D., M. Charlesworth, H. Dabies, J. MacKay, and V. Stott. 1997. Evaluating the effectiveness of educational innovations: Using the study process questionnaire to show that meaningful learning occurs. *Studies in Educational Evaluation* 23, no. 2: 141–57.

Kirschner, P., J. Sweller, and R. Clark. 2006. Why minimal guidance during instruction does not work: An analysis of the failure of constructivist, discovery, problem-based, experiential, and inquiry-based teaching. *Educational Psychologist* 41, no. 2: 75–86.

Kyndt, E., F. Dochy, E. Cascallar, and K. Struyven. 2011. The direct and indirect effect of motivation for learning on students' approaches to learning, through perceptions of workload and task complexity. *Higher Education Research and Development* 30, no. 2: 135–50.

Kyndt, E., F. Dochy, and H. Nijs. 2009a. Learning conditions for non-formal and informal workplace learning. *Journal of Workplace Learning* 21, no. 5: 369–83.

Kyndt, E., F. Dochy, M. Michielsen, and B. Moeyaert. 2009b. Employee retention: Organisational and personal perspectives. *Vocations and Learning* 2, no. 3: 195–215.

Kyndt, E., M. Michielsen, L. Van Nooten, S. Nijs and H. Baert. 2011. Learning in the second half of the career: Stimulating and prohibiting reasons for participation in formal learning activities. *International Journal of Lifelong Education,* in press.

Kyndt, E., F. Dochy, K. Struyven, and E. Cascallar. (submitted). Looking at learning approaches from the angle of student profiles. *Educational Psychology.*

Kyndt, E., F. Timmers, F. Dochy, and E. Cascallar. 2011. The effects of cooperative learning in real-life classrooms of performance, attitudes and perceptions: A meta-analysis. *Educational Research Review* (2011, submitted).

Lea, S., D. Stephenson, and J. Troy. 2003. Higher education students' attitudes to student-centred learning: Beyond 'educational bulimia'? *Studies in Higher Education* 28, no. 3: 321–34.

Marsick, V.J., and K. Watkins. 1990. *Informal and incidental learning in the workplace.* London: Routledge.

Mayer, R. 2004. Should there be a three-strikes rule against pure discovery learning? The case for guided methods of instruction *American Psychologist* 59, no. 1: 14–9.

Neilsen, A.C. 2000. Employer satisfaction with graduate skills: Research report. Evaluations and investigation programme. Canberra: DETYA, Higher Education Division. http://www.dest.gov.au/archive/highered%20/eippubs/eip99-/eip99_7pdf (accessed December 10, 2007).

Nijhuis, J., M. Segers, and W. Gijselaers. 2005. Influence of redesigning a learning environment on student perceptions and learning strategies. *Learning Environments Research* 8: 67–93.

Parker, P., D.T. Hall, and K.E. Kram. 2008. Peer coaching: A relational process for accelerating career learning. *Academy of Management Learning and Education* 7, no. 4: 487–503.

Parr, J.M., and M.A.R. Townsend. 2002. Environments, processes, and mechanisms in peer learning. *International Journal of Educational Research* 37: 403–23.

Pillay, H., G. Boulton-Lewis, and L. Wilss. 2003. Conceptions of work and learning at work: Impressions from older workers. *Studies in Continuing Education* 25, no. 1: 95–112.

Segers, M., J. Nijhuis, and W. Gijselaers. 2006. Redesigning a learning and assessment environment: The influence on students' perceptions of assessment demands and their learning strategies. *Studies in Educational Evaluation* 32: 223–42.

Smits, P., C. de Buisonjé, J. Verbeek, F. van Dijk, J. Metz, and O. ten Cate. 2003. Problem-based learning versus lecture-based learning in postgraduate medical education. *Scandinavian Journal of Work, Environment and Health* 29, no. 4: 280–7.

Struyven, K., F. Dochy, S. Janssens, and S. Gielen. 2006. On the dynamics of approaches to learning: The effects of the teaching/learning environment. *Learning and Instruction* 16, no. 4: 279–94.

Struyven, K., F. Dochy, S. Janssens, and S. Gielen. 2008. Students' experiences with contrasting learning environments: The added value of students' perceptions. *Learning Environments Research* 11: 83–109.

Topping, K. 1996. The effectiveness of peer tutoring in higher and further education: A typology and review of literature. *Higher Education* 32: 321–45.

Tynjälä, P. 1999. Towards expert knowledge? A comparison between a constructivist and a traditional learning environment in the university. *International Journal of Educational Research* 31, no. 5: 357–442.

Tynjälä, P. 2008. Perspectives into learning at the workplace. *Educational Research Review* 3, no. 2: 130–54.

Van den Bossche, P., W.H. Gijselaers, M. Segers, and P.A. Kirschner. 2006. Social and cognitive factors driving teamwork in collaborative learning environments: Team learning beliefs and behaviors. *Small Group Research* 37, no. 5: 490–521.

Vernon, D., and R. Blake. 1993. Does problem-based learning work?. A meta-analysis of evaluative research *Academic Medicine* 68, no. 7: 550–63.

Washer, P. 2006. Designing a system for observation of teaching. *Quality Assurance in Education* 14, no. 3: 243–50.

Wilson, J.M., P.S. Goodman, and M.A. Cronin. 2007. Group learning. *Academy of Management Review* 32: 1041–59.

A response from Japan to TLRP's ten principles for effective pedagogy

Tadahiko Abiko

Graduate School of Teacher Education, Waseda University, Tokyo, Japan

This article comments upon James and Pollard's contribution in comparison with perspectives on pedagogy in Japan, where the concept has tended to be discredited by academics. TLRP's clusters of 10 principles are reviewed and found to be persuasive and meaningful, especially in relation to the following points: the emphasis on recognising children's right to determine their future; the stress on 'empowering' rather than 'effectiveness' of school education; the valuing of abstract knowledge beyond the practical context; 'cautious optimism' about the potential to apply brain science to education; the unique value of 'scaffolding' in human learning; the proper role of self-evaluation by learners in assessment; the emphasis on making meaning in the interaction between internal desires and external context; the important role of 'Kizuna', i.e. human ties or bonds, as a variable mediating between achievement and the economic status of children; the essential function of 'informal education' out of school, especially the role of ICT; the emphasis on the importance of 'lesson study' in in-service education for teachers; and the argument for more decentralisation of educational administration to respond directly to people's voices. Japan should learn from this contribution in its search for effective pedagogy to support learning.

Some comments on the general framework and rationale

It is appropriate for me to begin my response to James and Pollard's contribution, in this volume, by commenting on the whole framework and overall rationale. For someone from Japan, James and Pollard provide an interesting and informative introduction to recent educational practice and research activities in England. The TLRP seems to be so inclusive and comprehensive that it stimulates the thought that we need to have a similar programme in Japan in order to connect practice effectively with research in education. In framing 10 principles for effective practice from their overview of the work, James and Pollard propose four clusters for consideration by practitioners and researchers, as well as among policy-makers. Such thematic clustering is valid and helpful.

In Japan, to date, the concept of 'pedagogy' has not attracted much attention, largely because it has been widely criticised. 'Pedagogy' (kyouiku-gaku) in Japanese is a general term for educational studies, including fields like history of education, ideals or philosophy of education, school education, adult education, higher education, comparative education, educational system and administration, educational management, sociology of education and psychology of education. Therefore, there is no debate about what 'pedagogy' is or should be as a whole. Instead, each research field within the overarching 'pedagogy' – educational studies – is discussed separately. If we need to discuss 'pedagogy' in Japan, in ways similar to the approach of James and Pollard, we do this as problems or issues of curriculum and instruction, didactics (kyouju-gaku) or teaching methods, school or classroom management and assessment. I use the term 'discuss' deliberately because in Japan, thus far, 'pedagogy' in this sense has been the subject of debate but not much empirical research. Idealistic or ideological discourses have been rather dominant in the Japanese educational research world. Partly for this reason, pedagogy has a rather dubious reputation. However, in the last 10 years, there has been a gradual change.

Another contrast between Japan and the UK is the view of children. In my country, most educationists are interested in what children have in common, not their individualities. Therefore, Brian Simon's words about what children have in common as members of the human species, quoted by James and Pollard, are very close to the Japanese view. However, given Simons' protestations about the lack of pedagogy in England, it is interesting that the study of 'pedagogy' or 'didactics' is not popular among academic researchers in Japan. Most Japanese scholars regard it as non-academic or non-scientific as a field of study, and its results are not thought to be sufficiently analytical, specific and effective.

Furthermore, many educational researchers in Japan choose not to use the terms 'effective' or 'effectiveness' in relation to pedagogy because they say these terms lack a humane, qualitative aspect. Similarly, they do not like the terms 'effective school' or 'effective teaching', which often implies, they think, that results are only measured quantitatively or superficially. Instead, some Japanese researchers prefer expressions like 'powerful' or 'empowering' schools, if translated in English (Shimizu 2009). In James and Pollard's contribution, the term 'effective' is used as in 'effective role of pedagogy'. This does not imply a need for quantitative measures; thus, it might be used appropriately and acceptably in a similar way in Japan because it is necessary to stress the need for evidence-based research in Japan too.

I find it curious, however, that 'effectiveness' is not linked to fulfilling the purpose of 'political socialisation'; instead, it is linked to the synergy of three aims: economic productivity, social cohesion and personal development. Most educationists in Japan have been interested in political socialisation as one of the principal purposes of education. As a member of the Central Council for Education of the Ministry of Education in Japan, I have met many politicians who are eager to link formal or public education directly to political goals. This, to me, seems to typify the relationship between education and governments in many countries. But James and Pollard do not mention political purposes in education in any direct way. The reason might be that the terms 'education' or 'pedagogy' are not restricted to school education in their contribution. Or, perhaps, throughout the history of education in Britain, political socialisation has not been so stressed as in Japan.

Comments on the clusters of principles

Educational values and purposes

Principle 1: Effective pedagogy equips learners for life in its broadest sense. It is persuasive that in this area three resources are mentioned: intellectual, personal and social. Here we find purposes like equity, social justice and the development of 'active citizens', in addition to 'economic development' and 'individual flourish (ing)'.

In Japan, the most valuable purpose of education is the whole development of character in each person. Of course we know that education by others is focused on helping a person grow up, or become independent, in any society of human beings. The meaning of 'independence', however, depends on time and place; it differs in different societies and in different periods of human history. At this time, in an increasing globalised environment, the emphasis is on lifelong education and especially 'to raise the ability of self-education'. Therefore, learning how to learn is crucial.

From this point of view, 'education' is differentiated from 'indoctrination' or 'brainwashing'. Learners, particularly children, have to be thought of not as dolls or robots to be controlled by teachers or parents, but as 'supreme rulers in future' (Abiko 2010b). We can educate them only to develop the ability to shape their own lives, after which we must leave them and disappear. It is today's children who will decide what society they should have. In this sense, we have to recognise they have 'the right to determine their future' and 'freedom to determine what kind of society they have in future'. We can communicate our hopes and desires for the future, but we cannot force them to become members of our envisioned future. There must be a clear distinction, therefore, between education and indoctrination, even when it is dressed up as 'political socialisation'.

Therefore, though political citizenship and economic development are necessary, instrumentally, to make every person 'independent' or 'blooming', the three purposes that James and Pollard mention are not equal, from an educational point of view. The synergy of the three must be productive to make every person, ultimately, free and independent from the present political and economic systems of our societies.

Curriculum, pedagogy and assessment

Under this heading, 'pedagogy' means almost the same as 'teaching methods or methodology'. Today teaching methods may include methods to promote learning by children at school as well as by adults outside school. It is very valuable to expand the meaning of 'pedagogy', as Paulo Freire attempted in his applications of the term to the adult world.

Principle 2: Effective pedagogy engages with valued forms of knowledge. Sociologists of knowledge have been very active in these last 10 or 20 years. Many of them have discussed political control of educational knowledge (Fujita 1997). In addition, postmodernists have claimed the value of school knowledge as relative, not absolute (Takahashi 1992). They emphasise that all knowledge is culturally and personally contextual, and they criticise the lack of acknowledgement of the contextuality of school knowledge in claims for the teaching of 'essential' theoretical knowledge.

However, we can also understand how abstract or theoretical knowledge connects with concrete life situations or daily contexts. It is valuable, then, to recognise that abstract knowledge can be free ('abstracted') from particular contexts or situations. But, in order to understand abstract knowledge properly, we must put it to practical use – apply it – in our daily problems so that we appreciate its value. I am sure that the 'infusion approach', described by James and Pollard, would not be successful without appreciation of the theoretical nature of the knowledge applied in the practical context. I am, therefore, somewhat concerned that 'context' in learning is stressed too much by James and Pollard, without equal emphasis on the conceptual aspects of knowledge to be learned. Abstraction is one of the strong points in 'knowledge'.

Many researchers have analysed categories of 'knowledge' and developed theoretical classifications. Moon and McCormick's criticism of Shulman's theory, referred to by James and Pollard, is particularly interesting and encourages us to think more about various kinds of knowledge. According to this analysis, the knowledge world consists of both an objective type of knowledge and a subjective type of knowledge. Knowledge can be objectively or subjectively organised in terms of the purpose of the knowledge-user. Numbers and letters are rather objective, but intentions and desires are very subjective. We must therefore acknowledge a sort of continuum of knowledge relativism in recognition of this.

As for the relationship between brain sciences and education, the authors properly claim that, 'although brain imaging techniques are giving fascinating results, the authors of a TLRP commentary in this field are sceptical of current brain-based applications'. In Japan, although there are very few educational researchers who refer to brain research results, it seems right, to me, that we should view with 'cautious optimism' the potential of brain research to be useful to educational theory and practice, in due course (Abiko 2002). I recall the words of Dr S. Tonegawa, a Japanese Nobel Prize neuroscientist in 1987, who told me a few years ago that brain scientists would not be able to engage with the field of education until they stopped using the terms 'stimulus' or 'information'. Knowledge and learning involve so much more. And, he added, we need 30 years of more work!

Principles 3 and 4: Effective pedagogy recognises the importance of prior experience and learning. Effective pedagogy requires learning to be scaffolded. It is surely important that teachers take account of learners' readiness or prior learning. Teachers need to try to identify various types of learners' mistakes or misconceptions in order to correct them and to promote learning activities. In this connection, James and Pollard mention Vygotsky's theory of the Zone of Proximal Development. In Japan, many researchers have been interested in ZPD theory, because, according to this view, the development of children depends not on maturity but on education. The scaffolding of learning is crucial in the learning of human beings. Among other animals, there is no scaffolding of learning, although some kinds of monkey, and New Caledonian crows, can learn how to use tools to get something to eat. Education through deliberate teaching activity is unique to human beings, so pedagogy, how to teach and teaching activities are found only in our species.

In addition, it is appropriate that 'dialogue' is stressed in classrooms as a means of scaffolding. Also in Japan, most contemporary educational researchers have stressed group learning in order to produce interaction and communication between pupils and teachers (Sato 1996). However, Japanese pupils have not been familiar with group activity in recent times, for Japanese families have few members: generally parents and one child or two. Young children do not, therefore, experience group activities often in their home lives. Despite this lack of 'out of school' experience, schoolteachers in Japan are expected to design group-learning activities intentionally for children at school.

Principle 5: Effective pedagogy needs assessment to be congruent with learning. It is surely vital that assessment should be linked to autonomous learning by pupils in order to promote it. For more than 30 years, one of my research activities has focused on pupil's self-evaluation or self-assessment. In my book entitled 'Self-Evaluation', published in 1987, I emphasised self-evaluation because of the emergence of 'lifelong learning' as an important educational goal (Abiko 1987). Lifelong learning requires the ability of self-evaluation if we are to continue autonomous learning throughout our whole lives.

Another of James and Pollard's suggestions is that pupil perspectives, strategies, relationships and identities are developed in assessment encounters. Thus, experiences of assessment should be considered as a social process and planned carefully with this in mind. Self-assessment must be linked to identity development as well. Kane's view, which they reference, that validity cannot be achieved by the manipulation of statistical models provides an important cautionary lesson. Validity fundamentally requires qualitative analysis and judgement, especially in relation to careful analysis of the multiplicity of teaching objectives. In the US, Wiggins and McTighe's concept of 'Backward Design' has become popular as part of a procedure of curriculum development called 'Understanding by Design' (Wiggins and McTighe 1998). This procedure could be useful to strengthen the alignment between assessment and curriculum, though there are very few schools that take account of this procedure in Japan.

Personal and social processes and relationships

Principle 6: Effective pedagogy promotes the active engagement of the learner. This principle should be universally recognised. Education should motivate children to engage with their learning enthusiastically. However, while being encouraged to engage autonomously with learning and independent study, students need to possess basic knowledge and skills to utilise as tools in order to think logically and discuss with others. Basic knowledge and skills, such as decoding and encoding text (basic reading and writing) and knowing number facts and how to calculate, have to be memorised or established by repetition and practice. Therefore, memorisation and inculcation of habits of mind and skill are to some extent essential, though this idea is often resisted, particularly, among Westerners. It is nevertheless possible and desirable to devise opportunities and methods for repetition and practice that children enjoy.

Similarly, emphasis on the social in 'construction of meaning in relation to circumstances' is a somewhat one-sided interpretation of making meaning; the other side of meaning making relates to the individual's internal, psychological processes. For example, the meaning of something can be connected with individual wants, desires and preferences as well as with social or cultural context. We sometimes interpret the meaning of something very subjectively from our own interests that are independent or separate from, often against or withstanding, social context. In other words, there is a danger in overestimating the validity of, or giving too much weight to, recent, popular propositions derived from sociology.

In Japan, sociology of education is now very influential in the educational research field. Thirty years ago, most Japanese researchers in education ignored sociologists of education because, in the main, they uncritically supported governmental policy. However, many contemporary sociologists of education now criticise governmental policy and administration, as have traditional pedagogical researchers of education. Therefore, Japanese research societies have increasingly accepted them as members, and the present president of the Japan Society for the Study of

Education, Professor H. Fujita, is a famous sociologist of education in Japan. In my opinion, it is proper that any sociologist of education is formally respected as a member of the educational research community, although this does not mean that the results of their research are indisputably reliable and valid.

Principle 7: Effective pedagogy fosters both individual and social processes and outcomes. This principle underlines the importance of group interaction as necessary and essential. It is therefore interesting, and surprising to me, that the authors are from England, where the one-to-one tutorial system, as exemplified in higher education in the Oxbridge colleges, was developed. In other countries, this is often regarded as a teaching style to be aspired to because of the opportunities it offers for individualised learning activity.

In Japan, much recent research in the socology of education shows that the economic condition of children's families correlates closely with achievement and the cultural well-being of children (Kariya 2002). Yet, only 30 years ago, Japanese sociologists said they could find no significant correlation between these variables. An alternative explanation for patterns of achievement might be found in the work of Professor K. Shimizu, a sociologist of education at Osaka University, who, 2 years ago, showed that 'Kizuna' in Japanese, i.e. ties or bonds, might have a more influential role in the academic achievement of children (Shimizu 2011). These ties or bonds are characterised by three variables: school refusal ratio (an indicator of friendship bonds); divorce ratio (an indicator of parental bonds); and ratio of home ownership (an indicator of ties to neighbours and community). This theory is much more persuasive than a simple association with economic status, because human resources are more important than economic resources in educational circumstances. These bonds and ties are a sort of 'social capital' that contributes to human learning activity because of the essential usefulness and benefits of human relationships.

Principle 8: Effective pedagogy recognises the significance of informal learning. This principle supports my own recent concerns about recognition of the importance of 'informal education' by the Japanese people. I strongly agree that 'informal learning out of school should be recognised as at least as significant as formal learning'. Informal learning and 'informal or social education' have been neglected in Japan, where most people express interest only in school or formal learning and education. Yet, ICT is very popular in informal learning contexts and offers opportunities to connect formal learning at school with informal learning out of school. However, the quality of the learning depends upon the quality of the software, and the way it is used to weave together both school culture and social context, as James and Pollard mention.

In Japan, there is much informal learning with ICT, but little 'informal or social education' of other kinds in most families and communities. Nowadays, Japanese people are overwhelmingly concerned with entrance examinations to good high schools and good universities. In order for their children to pass those examinations, they are mainly interested in 'schooling', in Ivan Illich's (1971) use of the word and in children's academic learning results. They do not regard informal education, at home and in the community, as very critical and crucial. Moreover, they mostly want someone, other than themselves, to educate their children.

In this context, ICT has been seen as 'a considerable threat to schooling practices', despite the possibilities for productive utilisation in classroom teaching and learning. Thus, informal learning with ICT is not well regarded in Japan, in terms of its educational potential, and 'informal education' out of school is almost dead, at home and in community. In Japanese schools, therefore, teachers are considered wholly responsible for children's education, including education out of school (through set homework or at crammers – 'juku') or in their families and communities. If, as James and Pollard argue, formal learning and education needs to connect with the informal learning and education at home or in community, parents need to be more involved (Lounsbury 2009). Children need informal education, at first by their parents, as a sort of base and protection. They feel lost and lonely if they cannot find some form of education at home, or parents' care as an expression of affection. Because parents cannot be replaced by others in the eyes of children, informal education by parents is essential and crucial. In recent years, I have urged Japanese parents to engage with the informal education of their children, in order to promote effective formal education at school (Abiko 2010b).

Teachers and policies

Principle 9: Effective pedagogy depends on the learning of all those who support the learning of others. James and Pollard are wise to stress the importance of life-long continuous learning of teachers through practice-based inquiry. In general, in Japan, we discuss this theme as 'in-service training', not as the lifelong learning of teachers. However, it is true that 'the development of supportive professional cultures within which teachers can learn' continuously through their practices 'is vitally important'. In my opinion, an orientation towards continuous professional learning is critical because teachers can idle away their time till someone, from outside the school, asks for a change. Therefore, teachers' culture and school atmosphere must support teachers' continuous learning, through both individual and institutional activities. At the current time in Japan, the government is very interested in developing in-service training programmes through all the life-stages of teachers.

Recently, Japanese Lesson Study has begun to attract attention from educationists across the world. In Japan, 'lesson study' has become a popular trend among teachers since the Second World War. They have criticised and evaluated their 'research lessons' with each other through observation of their practices, because this 'Problem-Solving method of New Education or Progressive Education' was relatively new to almost all Japanese teachers just after the Second World War (Shigematsu 1950). The concept of the 'research lesson' was originally from 'in-service education for teachers', while 'lesson study' is a research procedure and field proposed by academic educational researchers (Sunazawa 1964). Therefore, the 'research lesson' of in-service education has been incorporated into academic research activities with teachers' cooperation. Among Japanese researchers and teachers, any kind of study or research, whatever its focus, academic or practical, which involves the critique of 'research lessons', is called 'lesson study'. The purpose of lesson study is either to explain the principles of good instruction theoretically or to develop creative teaching practically. It is interesting that educationists abroad, some mentioned by James and Pollard, are drawn to 'lesson study' as a tool of in-service education. At this moment, in my country, 'lesson study', as academic research, is not so popular among researchers.

Principle 10: Effective pedagogy demands consistent policy frameworks with support for learning as their primary focus. This principle is crucial for policy-makers who often have difficulty understanding why educational initiatives and innovations take such a lot of time until their results are known. Therefore, we need 'sustainable' policy in the field of education, through establishing good partnerships or cooperative relationships between policy-makers and practitioners.

In Japan, we have had rather good ministries of education so far, because every minister has held the neutrality of formal or public education in high regard, despite his particular party political interests. As a result, the structures of formal education have not been so extremely biased by political ideology and administration in my country. Indeed, the present Democratic Party is thinking about decentralisation of educational administration in order to give more freedom to local authorities and schoolteachers to respond directly to the voices of parents and their children. Such a policy may be desirable if it provides more time for teachers to learn for their growth or development within the teaching profession (Abiko 2010a). In this context, it is again important to remember that informal learning has a crucial influence on formal learning and education. I want to insist that policy-makers take account of a wide range of educational and pedagogical aspects in the decisions they make, including evidence of the importance of both formal and informal learning. In today's world, we need to be concerned about informal learning and education, as never before.

As a whole, TLRP's 10 principles have stimulated me to reflect on school and informal education more deeply and deliberately. Individually, some of them are not as specific as I expected, but they are still informative and useful to our education in Japan. I am especially impressed that the words 'learning' and 'learners' are used throughout by James and Pollard. I agree that a consideration of learning activity is an essential prerequisite for pedagogy, teaching or education. Therefore, we must seek 'effective pedagogy as support for learning'.

References

Abiko, T. 1987. *Jiko-hyouka: Jiko-kyouiku-ron wo Koete (Self-evaluation: Beyond 'self-education' discourse)*. Tosho-bunka (in Japanese).
Abiko, T. 2010a. Issues of transformation in the ideas of curriculum reform, curriculum standards and textbooks: A Japanese perspective. *Journal of Textbook Research, 3*(1). Taiwan, ROC: National Institute for Compilation and Translation.
Abiko, T. 2010b. *'Kyouiku' no Joushiki Hi-joushiki ('Education': Thoughtful or thoughtless interpretation of formal and informal education)*. Gakubun-sha (in Japanese).
Abiko, T. 2002. Developmental stages and curriculum: A Japanese perspective. *Journal of Curriculum and Supervision* 17, no. 2: 160–70.
Fujita, H. 1997. *Kyouiku-kaikaku: Kyousei-jidai no Gakkou-dukuri (Educational reform: School making in symbiotic Era)*. Iwanami-shoten (in Japanese).
Illich, I. 1971. *Deschooling society*. New York: Harper and Row.

Kariya, T. 2002. *Kyouiku-kaikaku no Gensou (Illusion of educational reform)*. Chikuma-shinsho.

Lounsbury, J.H. 2009. Deferred but not deterred: A middle school manifesto. *Middle School Journal,* 40, no. 5: 31–6.

Sato, M. 1996. *Karikyuramu no Hihyou (Criticism on curriculum)*. Seori-shobou (in Japanese).

Shigematsu, T. 1950. *Kyouiku no Kagakuka (Scientification of education)*. Nara-josi-daigaku Fuzoku-shougakkou Gakushu-kenkyuukai (in Japanese).

Shimizu, K. 2009. *'Chikara no Aru' Gakkou no Tankyu (Inquiry for 'empowering' school)*. Osaka: Osaka University Press(in Japanese).

Shimizu, K., ed. 2011. *Kakusa wo Koeru Gakkou-dukuri (School making beyond the various gaps)*. Osaka: Osaka University Press (in Japanese).

Sunazawa, K., ed. 1964. *Kouza:Jugyou-kenkyu 5: Jugyou no Soshikika to Kenshou (Series: Lesson study 5: Systematization and verification of lesson)*. Meiji-tosho (in Japanese).

Takahashi, M. 1992. Gakkou-kyouiku no Paradaimu Tenkan (Paradigm Shift of School Education). *Paradaimu Shifuto 3: Han'ei to Yutakasa no Chihei (Paradigm shift 3: The horizon of prosperity and affluence)*. Fujisawa City Education and Culture Center (in Japanese).

Wiggins, G., and J. McTighe. 1998. *Understanding by design*. Boston, MA: ASCD.

Yes Brian, at long last, there is pedagogy in England – and in Singapore too. A response to TLRP's *Ten Principles for Effective Pedagogy*

David Hogan

National Institute of Education, Singapore

James and Pollard appropriately insist that the articulation of general, 'evidence-informed' pedagogical *principles* that can inform teacher judgments and policy-makers rather than detailed instructional *prescriptions* that tell teachers what to do is the most useful way to improve classroom practice at scale. This is surely right: teaching and learning are deeply contextual and highly contingent. Certainly, our experience in Singapore strongly supports this claim, particularly if backed up by appropriately designed *in situ*, iterative, authentic and extended professional learning experiences. Moreover, the specific generative principles that James and Pollard identify are substantial and important. However, I am not convinced, given my experience in Singapore and my understanding of research findings more generally, that the principles they isolate are either adequately specified or jointly sufficient to optimise improving the quality of teaching and learning in British schools. But certainly what James and Pollard, and the TLRP team more generally, have achieved makes a unique and significant contribution to that effort and to the broader international movement to design and deliver educational research that is rigorous, relevant and useful.

Introduction

At the very beginning of *Ten Principles for Effective Pedagogy*, Mary James and Andrew Pollard quote Brian Simon's lament from 1981, 'Why is there no pedagogy in England?' (Simon 1981) in which he compared the multidisciplinary and scientific tradition of pedagogic thought and practice in Europe focused on the articulation of evidence-informed 'general principles' of teaching and learning (including 'didactics') with the more instrumental, pragmatic and ideologically susceptible approach to teaching that he found in England. Simon believed that pedagogy – the act and discourse of teaching – was in England neither coherent, systematic nor evidence based and that English educators had developed nothing comparable to the continental European 'science of teaching'. Simon published a second essay (Simon 1994) that restated and updated his 1981 essay, and the debate continued on its merry way, culminating in a brilliant polemic by Robin Alexander in 2004 that rejoined the issue again in a withering critique of the continuing ideological orientation of official pedagogical discourse in England, with its preoccupation with top-down control, 'competence, excellence and failure' combined with a call for an informed analytical account of pedagogy (Alexander 2004).

James and Pollard forthrightly locate TLRP's *Ten Principles for Effective Pedagogy* in the European rather than the British pedagogical tradition. Although they are far from being uninterested in individual differences, they insist that the more pressing imperative is the articulation of general, 'evidence-informed' pedagogical *principles* that can inform teacher judgments and policy-makers rather than detailed instructional *prescriptions* that tell teachers what to do. This is surely right: teaching and learning are deeply contextual and highly contingent and classrooms inherently problematic, messy, indeterminate, fluid, unpredictable and non-standardised (Darling Hammond 1996, 69–70). Certainly, our experience in Singapore strongly indicates that improving teaching does not so much depend on developing and imposing prescriptive pedagogical algorithms, or converting teachers to a sectarian pedagogical creed (whether direct instruction, active construction, teaching for understanding, constructivism or social constructivism), but providing them with well-supported generative principles that can inform and guide the contextualized judgments of teachers, particularly if backed up by appropriately designed in situ, iterative, authentic and extended professional learning experiences (Hogan 2011). Indeed, John Hattie (2009) suggests that such generative principles can be reduced to one fundamental pedagogical principle – visible teaching and learning.[1] This is a little too minimalist for my liking, but the more general point is well taken. Consequently, I am deeply sympathetic to the argument that the development of generative general principles rather than the imposition of prescriptive algorithms is far more likely to improve the quality of teaching and learning. Moreover, the specific generative principles that James and Pollard identify are substantial and important, although I am not convinced, given my experience in Singapore and my understanding of research findings more generally, that the principles they isolate are either adequately specified or jointly sufficient to optimise improving the quality of teaching and learning in British schools. But certainly what James and Pollard, and the TLRP team more generally, have achieved makes a unique and significant contribution to that effort and to the broader international movement to design and deliver educational research that is rigorous, relevant and useful (Hogan, Teh, and Dimmock 2011).

Singapore's CRPP *vis-a-vis* UK's TLRP

In March 2003, the Singapore government established the Centre for Research in Pedagogy and Practice (CRPP) in Singapore's sole teacher training and educational research institution, the National Institute of Education (NIE), with an initial five-year grant about half the size of the TLRP grant. CRPP initially pursued, and has continued to pursue, five key objectives:

(1) to describe and measure the patterns of classroom pedagogy in Singaporean schools;
(2) to measure the impact of pedagogical practices on student outcomes controlling for student characteristics;
(3) to design technologically enriched learning environments and support their integration into classroom pedagogy;
(4) to identify opportunities for the improvement in pedagogical practice through a carefully designed and evidence-based intervention strategy; and

(5) to support evidence-based policy formulation and instructional practice to meet the challenges of twenty-first-century institutional environments.

Two years later, the Ministry established a second research centre at NIE, the Learning Sciences Laboratory (LSL), to support the more effective incorporation of ICT into classroom pedagogy. In 2008, the Ministry approved a second five-year grant and supported the establishment of an Office of Education Research within NIE with overall responsibility for developing and implementing a strategically focused, national research, development and innovation (RD&I) programme that built upon the findings of the first five years and took into account the Ministry's emerging policy priorities, international research findings and the changing institutional landscape of education in Singapore and internationally (Hogan 2011). My own research has focused for the past seven years on measuring, mapping and modelling classroom instruction and student outcomes using large national samples of schools, students and teachers and employing both quantitative and qualitative methodologies.

If Brian Simon had been able to visit Singapore in 2003, he might well have asked, 'Why is there no pedagogy in Singapore?' Prior to 2003, and even later, pedagogical discourse in Singapore was heavily statist and top-down, dominated by Ministry of Education (MOE) policy pronouncements and programmes and by a tradition of centralised control of pedagogical policy and practice. In addition, for complex institutional reasons, the NIE had not been successful in articulating a counter-hegemonic pedagogy, although it was far from homogenous in its pedagogical views internally. On top of this, professional organisations in Singapore were, and continue to be, historically weak or non-existent, particularly at the subject level, although it is fair to say the teachers themselves have held a diverse range of views about pedagogical matters. Indeed, many teachers believe that the institutional rules governing schooling in Singapore (particularly those associated with Singapore's national high stakes assessment system) inhibit their ability to teach in the way they would have liked (Hogan 2011). Still, over the past decade, the system has been willing, cautiously and incrementally, to support pedagogical innovation, but for the most part it has been very diffident about tinkering with the major institutional rules that shape pedagogical discourse and practice. But while it is true that Singapore's pedagogical discourse has, historically speaking, been highly statist and preoccupied with 'competence, excellence and failure', it is not true that it lacks 'coherence, systematicity or purposefulness', as Simon and Alexander charged British pedagogy. Indeed, one of the hallmarks of Singapore's pedagogical regime is its very clear purposefulness, its considerable systematicity, its pedagogical pluralism at the level of practice, its obvious coherence institutionally and its pragmatism and lack of sectarianism in matters of pedagogical creed. Instead, its principal problems lie elsewhere.

The logic of TLRP's Ten Principles

James and Pollard write that:

> ... a major ambition of the TRLP Programme, for both analytic and impact purposes, has been to try to produce an evidence-informed statement of 'general principles' of teaching and learning, just as Simon advocated. The basic view is that a great deal is

actually known about pedagogy, both in the UK and internationally, but that the synthesis, communication and implementation of such knowledge are far weaker than they should be. (James and Pollard 2011, in this volume)

They go on to indicate that 'the diverse nature of TLRP's projects, which focused on different research questions in different contexts, sometimes using different methods and theoretical perspectives, did not permit formal quantitative meta-analysis, rendering aggregated effect sizes of interventions as indicators of "what works"'. Instead, 'each project engaged with existing research in its own particular field or sub-field and built on this to take knowledge forward cumulatively'. Moreover:

> ...the expectation that the research would be carried out in authentic settings made it impossible to control all the variables operating at any one time. But it enabled researchers, working with practitioners, to grapple with the issues of implementation that so often confound best efforts to 'scale up' promising innovations. Furthermore, it enabled practitioners to use their knowledge, of the features of particular settings and characteristics of learners, to develop and refine generalisations from the original research. (James and Pollard 2011, in this volume)

For all these reasons, they argue, they are not able to 'make unequivocal claims about findings in terms of categorical knowledge or cause–effect relationships'. What they could do instead was 'to offer "evidence-informed principles", which could engage with diverse forms of evidence while calling for the necessary application of contextualized judgement by teachers, practitioners and/or policy-makers'. Such principles, they believed, 'could enable the accumulation and organisation of knowledge in resilient, realistic and practically useful ways and had the potential,

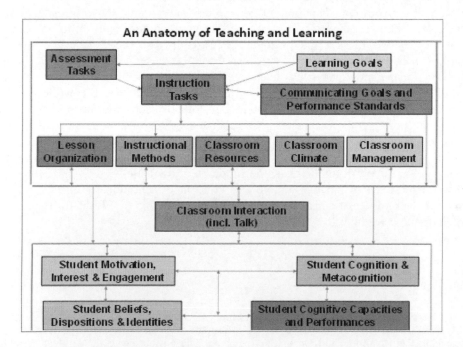

Figure 1.   Core 2: an anatomy of teaching and learning.

progressively, to generate understanding and language for use within public debates' (James and Pollard 2011, in this volume).

In developing its ten principles, the TLRP team developed an iterative 'analytical and synthetic approach to reviewing the TLRP evidence' in the light of the 'conceptual map that TLRP had developed to represent the scope of its interests with reference to teaching and learning' (see Figure 1 in James and Pollard 2011, in this volume). This approach strikes me as reasonable enough, given the overall design of the TLRP programme. But their approach does involve some analytical opportunity costs, because the scope of the principles of teaching and learning they identify is methodologically dependent on the projects that *happened* to be funded by the TLRP programme. This seems to me unfortunate, since there are many important areas of research that happened *not* to be funded by the TLRP. This has limited their opportunity to identify other important 'evidence-informed general principles' that I think research suggests need attention. This would have mattered less if James and Pollard had attempted to position TLRP's *Ten Principles For Effective Pedagogy* in a broader normative framework that mapped out in a systematic way what additional collateral principles have been well supported by research internationally. Without that broader framework, well-intentioned (but relatively uninformed) practitioners and policy-makers might well conclude that the only principles that they need to attend to are those identified by the TLRP programme. In effect, while these are important principles, it is not at all clear to me that the *Ten Principles* by themselves constitute a sufficiently comprehensive pedagogical framework capable of framing pedagogical decision-making at the classroom level and policy-making at the government level in a way that optimises the capacity of the TLRP to enhance the quality of teaching and learning in the UK.

In Singapore, CRPP adopted a different approach to the design of its research programme and the development of similar kinds of principles. Given the absence of any systematic nationwide data on what happened in Singaporean classrooms and what impact classroom practices had on student outcomes at the time CRPP was established in 2003, CRPP decided to focus, in both the first and second round of funding, on supporting comprehensive baseline data projects that measured, mapped and modelled classroom practices, processes and student outcomes (what we called the Core research programme), and to use the findings from this research to identify aspects of classroom practice and student learning that would benefit from targeted, intervention or innovations. At the same time, we also supported an additional intervention programme based on strong but not systematic evidence, and a programme to support the development and integration of cutting edge technologies in the classroom. The current research programme, now in its third year, includes a second-generation Core research programme, launched at the beginning of 2010, that covers much the same territory analytically but is much more focused theoretically because it has been able to draw on the results of the Core 1 programme to identify areas for further investigation and develop hypotheses for testing (Hogan 2011).

So far, CRPP's overall strategy has had mixed results. The Core 1 (2003–2005) and Core 2 (2010–2012) baseline research programmes have produced good and useful data that have had a considerable impact on policy-making and programme development. Some interventions, both experimental design research and design research, were well designed and effective but proved hard to sustain and difficult to scale up. Other interventions proved not to be well designed, effective, sustainable or scalable. Some interventions in technology have proved highly imaginative, effective and capable of incorporation into classroom pedagogy. Overall, the quality of our research has been reasonable, our conference participation and publication rates are way up and we are now at a point where we are able to identify with some confidence, the character, logic, internal variation, alignment and effectiveness of the instructional system in Singaporean classrooms. We are even at a point where we have been able to generate an initial statement of 'evidence-informed' principles of teaching and learning (and effective implementation and teacher learning) that is sensitive to the Singapore context. Notwithstanding these achievements, however, we are a long way yet from being able to say that we have found our particular pedagogical Holy Grail (Hogan 2011).

Curriculum values and purposes

The first of the ten principles that James and Pollard identify focuses on the broad objectives of the school curriculum:

PRINCIPLE 1: Effective pedagogy equips learners for life in its broadest sense.

Principle 1 offers a clear, capacious, decidedly liberal but very general conception of education that self-consciously, and appropriately, distances itself from narrow performative measures of student achievement of the kind encouraged by neo-liberal or high stakes assessment regimes. James and Pollard report that the origins of this particular principle lie in thematic group deliberations and commissioned work from the Philosophy of Education Society of Great Britain. But while this formulation is very appealing, it is exceedingly general and de-contextualized. In particular, I would have preferred to see it grounded in an intellectual history of educational policy and philosophical reflection in the UK and a considered account of changes in the institutional environment that are profoundly transforming the kinds of skills, understandings, dispositions and identities that young people will need to successfully negotiate twenty-first-century institutional settings and the contemporary existential condition. Moreover, because of its generality, it is difficult to see how it could possibly inform curriculum planning and instructional practice at the classroom level, including giving teachers analytical purchase on the kinds of skills, understandings, dispositions and identities that twenty-first-century students need. My experience in Singapore is that to give teachers this kind of purchase they need access to a conception of pedagogy that focuses not on the transmission, accumulation and reproduction of school knowledge but on domain-specific and transdisciplinary forms of *complex knowledge construction, communication, justification and application* (Hogan 2011).

Curriculum, pedagogy and assessment

Under the rubric of curriculum, pedagogy and assessment, James and Pollard identify four principles generated by the TLRP programme:

PRINCIPLE 2: Effective pedagogy engages with valued forms of knowledge.

PRINCIPLE 3: Effective pedagogy recognizes the importance of prior experience and learning.

PRINCIPLE 4: Effective pedagogy requires learning to be scaffolded.

PRINCIPLE 5: Effective pedagogy needs assessment to be congruent with learning.

These principles are legitimate and well supported evidentially. Still, to my mind, they do not fully exhaust the relevant foundational pedagogical principles that ought come into play here.

Principle 2 – *Effective pedagogy engages with valued forms of knowledge* – is an immensely important principle and attests to the continued effort to 'bring knowledge back in' to curriculum debates that a chastened Michael Young (Young 2008) wrote about some years ago. James and Pollard are right to emphasise it, as we have in Singapore, although we have paid considerably more attention to the nature of the knowledge work or practices that students engage in classrooms than TLRP appears to have done. In particular, we have focused a lot of analytical attention on the intellectual quality of the instructional and assessment tasks that students are asked to work on, and the extent to which the knowledge practices they engage in are informed by, and are consistent with, domain-specific forms of disciplinary knowledge work and epistemic norms. Indeed, we have come to the conclusion that along with the careful specification and communication of learning goals and assessment standards at the lesson and unit level, the design of instructional and assessment tasks is the fundamental determinant of the quality of teaching and learning in the classroom and that all else – the selection of instructional methods, the social organisation of the lesson, classroom learning environment, classroom management, even (much to my surprise) classroom interaction and talk – are derivative and secondary (see Figure 1). Of course, this is not a unique or an original finding. Newmann, Bryk, and Nagaok (2001, 31), for example, reflecting on their work in the Annenberg Chicago schools reform project, concluded that the key to securing high-quality learning outcomes depends not on the selection of instructional methods but on the construction of high-quality instructional tasks: 'We wish to emphasize . . .[that] no particular teaching practice or strategy assures that students will undertake work that makes high-quality intellectual demands on them. . . *Our key point is that it is the intellectual demands embedded in classroom tasks, not the mere occurrence of a particular teaching strategy or technique, that influence the degree of student engagement and learning*'. So too John Hattie in *Visible Learning*: 'It is what teachers get students to do in the class that emerged as the strongest component of the accomplished teacher's repertoire, rather than what the teacher, specifically does'. (Hattie 2009, 35)

Principle 3 – *Effective pedagogy recognizes the importance of prior experience and learning* – is an important and well-established constructivist principle. But learning scientists generally regard it as but one of a number of interrelated learning principles that need to be attended to. Linda Darling Hammond, for example, drawing on the research of John Bransford and others, recently suggested that there is a broad research consensus regarding the fundamental importance of three learning principles to successful learning and understanding:

(1) Students come into the classroom with *prior knowledge and preconceptions about how the world works* that must be addressed and engaged if students are to understand new concepts and information.

(2) To develop competence in an area of inquiry, students must: (a) have a deep foundation of factual knowledge; and (b) organise and use knowledge *conceptually if they are to understand it meaningfully, retrieve it and apply it effectively beyond the classroom.*

(3) Students learn more effectively if they understand how they learn and how to manage their own learning, including learning to take control of their own learning by defining learning goals and monitoring their progress in achieving them (*'metacognitive wisdom' and self-regulation*) (Darling Hammond et al. 2008, 3–4).

In our work in Singapore, we have been highly impressed by the intellectual strength and utility of this essentially constructivist model of learning, although I am convinced that they need to be supplemented with additional statements on the nature of understanding and the interaction between procedural knowledge and conceptual understanding, the role that drill and practice and memorisation can play in the development of understanding, and the importance of situated cognition and cognitive apprenticeships to the development of expertise and engaging students in knowledge tasks that focus on complex knowledge construction, communication, justification and application.

Principle 4 – *Effective pedagogy requires learning to be scaffolded* – is by now a well-established principle of teaching and learning that can be traced to the work of Vygotsky, Bruner and Wood, and sociocultural learning theory generally. Importantly, James and Pollard include the work of Robin Alexander and others on 'enacting dialogue' as a key form of scaffolding (James and Pollard 2011, in this volume) although they do not explicitly link it to research on active teaching and teaching for understanding with which it is now often connected (see, for example, Good and Brophy 2008, chaps. 9–11). My principal reservation, again reflecting my experience in Singapore and understanding of the international research literature, is that their account does not sufficiently emphasise that to be effective scaffolding needs to be proceeded by close monitoring of student learning (or as Hattie would have it, feedback from the student to the teacher) for otherwise the teacher is not in a position to know when and when not to scaffold and ought to be followed by feedback from the teacher to the student (that is, formative assessment) in order to maximise student learning gains (Black and Wiliam 1998; Hattie 2009, chap. 9). Although James and Pollard do discuss formative assessment/assessment for learning (AfL) in the context of Principle 5, it is also important pedagogically to link AfL to scaffolding more directly.

In their discussion of Principle 5 – *Effective pedagogy needs assessment to be congruent with learning* – James and Pollard focus on current efforts to enhance the validity of student assessments after decades of psychometric preoccupation with issues of reliability. Specifically, they conclude that, '*Assessment should be designed and implemented with the goal of achieving maximum validity both in terms of learning outcomes and learning processes. It should help to advance learning as well as determine whether learning has occurred*'. It is hard not to agree with this, but it is a lot easier said than done, and it does not capture all the issues that we have found we have had to struggle with in Singapore where the national high stakes assessments (NHSA) at the end of primary school (year 6), the end of secondary school (year 10) and the end of year 12 exert substantial institutional as well as pedagogical influence on classroom practice. By virtue of the tight nexus between social mobility patterns and national high stakes assessments, and the commitment of the government to 'meritocratic' sorting and allocation through the NHSA, reliability remains the overriding issue for parents and the government. This constrains the ability of the system to develop assessments that have greater twenty-first-century institutional authenticity and validity, or to support school-based high stakes assessment, even as a component of the overall NHSA system. At the same time, it is very clear to us and to teachers themselves that the character and logic of classroom instruction is directly shaped by NHSA – in Singapore, as they do elsewhere, teachers teach to the test – and that this constrains the opportunity and willingness of teachers to probe issues in depth or to focus on the development of complex knowledge understandings, skills and dispositions required by twenty-first-century institutional environments. In effect, although it places a floor on student learning, the NHSA system in Singapore places a ceiling on it as well. For some time I thought the solution to this imbroglio was to shift to a (partial) school-based NHSA system. I still think that this needs to be part of the solution, but that by itself it is insufficient. What also needs to happen, given the tight institutional nexus between social mobility and the NHSA system and the broader cultural understandings and institutional rules that define education in Singapore, is a clear commitment to improving the quality and authenticity – the validity – of the assessment tasks that students work on in their NHSA. Because they teach to the test, teachers will inevitably and very quickly adjust their semestral assessments and their instructional tasks accordingly (Hogan 2011). Failing this, I do not have much hope that authenticity and validity considerations will trump credentialing and reliability considerations in Singapore.

In general then, our research findings support TLRP's curriculum, pedagogy and assessment principles although I think they are underspecified and insufficiently integrated into a more fully developed account of instructional practice and principles. I appreciate that their methodological approach limited the generation of evidence-informed general principles to the specific research projects supported by TLRP. But the danger of this approach, as I indicated earlier, is that some end-users might be tempted to conclude that TLRP's Ten Principles are all that they particularly need to attend to in order to improve the quality of teaching and learning in the UK. In my view, that is unlikely to be the case.

In Singapore, as I also indicated earlier, we have approached this challenge in a different way (Hogan 2011). What we have attempted to do in Singapore is conceptually frame instruction as a hierarchical, dynamic *instructional system* requiring the appropriate selection and iterative alignment and realignment of learning goals, instructional and assessment tasks, lesson organisation, instructional methods, classroom learning environment and management, and classroom talk (see Figure 1). We have also measured (using both quantitative and qualitative approaches), mapped and modelled statistically the pattern and logic of classroom instruction in Singapore and their impact on a broad array of student outcomes (including motivation, engagement, self-beliefs, identity formations, cognitive achievement and meta-cognitive self-regulation) controlling for family background and individual characteristics. It is on the basis of these findings, positioned within a broad account of international research findings, that we have attempted to generate our judgements about what changes to instructional practice need to be prioritized. Moreover, we have attempted to position these judgements within a broad, hybridized *pedagogical* framework that draws on elements of active teaching, direct instruction, traditional instruction and, above all, on a broad and expansive understanding of the teaching for understanding framework (Good and Brophy 2008; Wiggins and McTighe 2005; Galton 2007; Newmann et al. 1997; Darling Hammond et al. 2008; Wiske 1998; Cohen, McLaughlin, and Talbert 1993). This demonstrates institutional validity and cultural viability in the Singapore context and enhances the ability of teachers to frame their own instructional practices conceptually and theoretically in a comprehensive, coherent and principled way.

Personal and social processes and relationships

The third set of principles James and Pollard identify focus on personal and social processes and relationships:

> *PRINCIPLE 6: Effective pedagogy promotes the active engagement of the learner.*

> *PRINCIPLE 7: Effective pedagogy fosters both individual and social processes and outcomes.*

> *PRNCIPLE 8: Effective pedagogy recognizes the significance of informal learning.*

Again, I have no difficulty with these principles – each of them is well supported by international research findings as well as by TLRP findings. Our own research in Singapore supports principles very similar to these as well. However, there are some relatively minor differences of emphasis between TLRP's proposals and our proposals in Singapore. For the most part, these reflect quite different institutional landscapes in the two countries. With respect to Principles 6 and 7, for example, we found that Singaporean students are, relatively speaking, already highly engaged in their school work, that teachers in Singapore across the board, contrary to our initial expectations, are far more likely to rely on mastery achievement norms than competitive norms, and that teachers already employ, again contrary to our expectations, a wide range of instructional practices drawing on what are, in theory, quite different pedagogical traditions – traditional instruction, direct instruction, active construction, teaching for understanding, and even, to our considerable surprise, co-regulated learning strategies. Indeed, given the degree of covariance between instructional practices in Singapore, we have come to understand that instructional practice is inclusive, non-sectarian and hybridized and that this is one of the great strengths of classroom instruction in Singapore. This is not to say that there is no room for improvement in classroom practice – there is. We found, for example, that there is very little high-quality collaborative group work, although lots of what we term pseudo-group work where students sit in a group together but are not engaged in interdependent, collaborative group tasks. We also found that teachers are not especially good at communicating learning goals and the criteria and standards of high-quality work – forms of communication that are vital to what we term, following John Hattie, visible teaching and learning. We did not find much evidence that teachers attend to the task of designing instructional and assessment tasks focused on complex knowledge construction, communication, justification or application or, indeed, that they spend much time in lesson planning at all. We have not yet found much evidence that instructional practices are strategically chosen rather than tactically deployed, well aligned rather than loosely coupled, or principled rather than pragmatic and opportunistic, although not all of the evidence is in yet so I reserve the right to change my judgment in this matter. Nor, finally, have we found nearly enough evidence of what Barnes and Mercer (Mercer and Hodgkinson 2008) called 'exploring talk', and we term 'understanding talk', which focuses on clarifying and/ or developing meaning, explaining reasons, making connections, identifying and applying relevant domain-specific epistemic standards, framing and reframing issues, or dialogical 'cumulation', to use Robin Alexander's term (Alexander 2008). Indeed, many of our specific proposals to improve the quality of teaching and learning focus on exactly these issues, but conceptualised not as discrete 'principles' but integrated into a broad teaching for understanding framework.

Teachers and policy

The final set of 'evidence-informed' principles that James and Pollard identify focus on professional and organisational learning:

> *PRINCIPLE 9: Effective pedagogy depends on the learning of all those who support the learning of others.*

> *PRINCIPLE 10: Effective pedagogy demands consistent policy frameworks with support for learning as their primary focus.*

Yet again, I have no particular issue with these principles, given that the research findings, including our own in Singapore, strongly support them. The only differences are those of emphasis rather than substance. In the development of our approach to professional learning in Singapore, I have grown increasingly despairing of conventional forms of professional development focused upon workshop participation and action research forms of instructional improvement; in our experience, both appear to have limited sustainable impacts on classroom instruction. In addition, I have grown increasingly sceptical of the utility of most efforts to translate university research findings into practical algorithms – teaching is simply too contextual, too contingent, too complex, and teachers generally too busy, for this strategy to pay off. Instead, I am now far more inclined to support *in situ* forms of professional development that occurs in small professional learning communities (5–6 staff) in schools led by an expert non-executive teacher working together on priority innovations that are evidence-based, of high value, highly scaffolded and extended over time (3–5 years). These de-privatise instruction, make visible implicit beliefs and assumptions, and foster rich professional analysis and reflection. The *Keeping Learning on Track* programme, focused on the relationship between formative assessment and instruction, supported by ETS and led by Dylan Wiliam in the US, is a good example of what I have in mind (Thompson and Wiliam 2008). Otherwise, given the complex multimodal (bureaucratic, professional, cultural, institutional, ideological, symbolic) structure of instructional governance and the ingrained collective pedagogical *habitus* of teachers in Singapore, it is unlikely that significant and sustainable changes in instructional practice are achievable. Indeed, these considerations, plus the system's reliance (until recently) on conventional workshop and action research initiatives, help explain why teachers still teach now in much the same way they did six years ago when we last measured instructional practices in the Core 1 programme.

Conclusion

One of the most persistent criticisms of educational research in most Western countries for many decades has been its irrelevance and its lack of utility to policy-makers and practitioners in schools. In particular, critics have complained that educational research has been rather more preoccupied with arcane theoretical debates (or the professional ambitions of academics) than making a difference in the classroom or decision-making forums; that it has been highly diffuse in focus and uncoordinated in design and implementation; that too much of it has been of mediocre quality and/or relied on small unrepresentative samples; that when it does focus on interventions it focused all too often on interventions that are not sustainable, scalable or fundable; that it all too often ignored the practical, tacit classroom knowledge of teachers or failed to develop intervention models that conceptualised teachers as co-constructors and professional partners rather than implementers of pre-planned intervention programmes; and that it failed to invest significantly in building individual, institutional and organisational capacity and developing sustainable institutional arrangements, practices and networks.

Of course, not all of the criticism has been fair or balanced, but there is more than a little merit in many of the criticisms. In my view, and from this distance, TLRP, and the *Ten Principles for Effective Pedagogy*, has made a substantial effort to addressing these challenges in both the UK and international contexts. While I clearly have some reservations about some issues, on balance TLRP and the *Ten Principles* address major problematics in teaching and learning that are central to the concerns of policy-makers and teachers internationally. Indeed, while the official discourse of successive Conservative, Labour and Coalition Governments has continued to stress compliance, pragmatism and ideology, TLRP, along with Robin Alexander's Cambridge Primary Review (Alexander 2009), gives one reason to hope that there is, some thirty years after Brian Simon asked his incendiary question, a rich discourse about pedagogy in Britain that is not beholden to an overweening state and its ideological mercenaries.

Notes

1. 'The teacher must know when learning is correct or incorrect; learn when to experiment and learn from the experience; learn to monitor, seek and give feedback; and know to try alternative learning strategies when others do not work,' Hattie writes. 'What is most important is that teaching is visible to the student, and that learning is visible to the teacher. The more the student becomes the teacher and the more teacher becomes the student, then the more successful are the outcomes' (Hattie (2009), 25).

References

Alexander, R. 2004. Still no pedagogy? Principle, pragmatism and compliance in primary education *Cambridge Journal of Education* 34, no. 1: 7–33.

Alexander, R. 2008. *Essays on pedagogy.* London: Routledge.

Alexander, R., ed. 2009. *Children, their world, their education: Final report and recommendations of the Cambridge primary review.* London: Routledge.

Black, P., and D. Wiliam. 1998. Assessment and classroom learning. *Assessment in Education: Principles, Policies and Practice* 5, no. 1: 7–57.

Cohen, D., M. McLaughlin, and J. Talbert, eds. 1993. *Teaching for understanding: Challenges for policy and practice.* San Francisco: Jossey-Bass.

Darling Hammond, L., B. Barron, P.D. Pearson, A. Schoenfeld, E. Stage, T. Zimmerman, G. Cervetti, et al. 2008. *Powerful learning: What we know about teaching for understanding.* San Francisco: Jossey-Bass.

Darling Hammond, L. 1996. *The right to learn: A blueprint for creating schools that work.* San Francisco: Jossey-Bass.

Galton, M. 2007. *Learning and teaching in the primary classroom.* London: Sage.

Good, T., and J. Brophy. 2008. *Looking in classrooms.* Boston: Pearson/Allyn and Bacon.

Hattie, J. 2009. *Visible learning: A synthesis of over 800 meta-analyses relating to achievement.* London: Routledge.

Hogan, D. 2011. *Interim report: Core 1 and 2 research program.* 3 vol. Singapore: National Institute of Education.

Hogan, D., L.W. Teh, and C. Dimmock. 2011. Educational knowledge mobilization and utilization in Singapore. Paper prepared for the 2011 conference of the international alliance of leading educational institutions, June, OISIE, Toronto.

James, M., and A. Pollard. 2011. TLRP's ten principles for effective pedagogy: Rationale, development, evidence, argument and impact. *Research Papers in Education* 26, no. 3: 275–326.

Mercer, N., and S. Hodgkinson, eds. 2008. *Exploring talk in school.* London: Sage.

Newmann F. Associates. 1997. *Authentic achievement: Restructuring schools for intellectual quality.* San Francisco: Jossey-Bass.

Newmann, F., A. Bryk, and J. Nagaoka. 2001. *Authentic intellectual work and standardized tests: Conflict or coexistence.* Chicago: Consortium on Chicago School Research.

Simon, B. 1981. Why no pedagogy in England? In *Education in the eighties: The central issues*, ed. B. Simon and W. Taylor, 124–45. London: Batsford.

Simon, B. 1994. *The state and educational change: Essays in the history of education and pedagogy.* London: Lawrence and Wishart.

Thompson, M., and D. Wiliam. 2008. Tight but loose: A conceptual framework for scaling up reform. In *Tight but loose: Scaling up teacher professional development in diverse contexts*, ed. E.C. Wylie. Princeton, NJ: Educational Testing Service.

Wiggins, G., and J. McTighe. 2005. *Understanding by design,* 2nd ed. Alexandra, VA: ASCD.

Wiske, M.S., ed. 1998. *Teaching for understanding: Linking research with practice.* San Francisco: Jossey-Bass.

Young, M. 2008. *Bringing knowledge back in from social constructivism to social realism in the sociology of knowledge.* London: Routledge.

A response from Canada to TLRP's ten principles for effective pedagogy

Lorna Earl

Aporia Consulting Ltd. Toronto, Canada and University of Auckland, Auckland, New Zealand

The TLRP has provided a wealth of information that can form the foundation of conversations and debate for researchers, policymakers and practitioners. This paper focuses on two of the issues raised by James and Pollard: (1) the methodology that they used to analyse and synthesise the learning from massive amounts of data into a coherent and defensible set of interpretations, in order to address large and important questions about pedagogy and learning and to share their learning broadly; and (2) the difficult issue of 'Getting to the "spirit" of Assessment for Learning'.

Introduction

I have followed the work of the TLRP for a number of years and marvelled at the scope and depth of the investigations that make it up. The original aims seemed lofty and sometimes even unattainable (see Figure 1). This major series of intertwined studies and investigations has yielded mountains of data with the potential to generate many important insights about learning, teaching, assessment and educational change. On occasion, I wondered how this diverse group of researchers would ever manage the massive amounts of data and actually make it accessible for others to use in policy and practice. This paper by James and Pollard has provided an image of both the journey and the learning that has emerged from the synergy among the members of the research team that has been channelled and fostered throughout the ten years of the project, as they have shared what they were learning with one another, mined the data for bigger issues and made their learning available to others around the world. In my response to the contribution from James and Pollard, in this volume, I have selected two issues to examine and offer comments upon. These issues are ones that I have pondered and found both challenging and interrelated in my own work. I thank the authors and the TLRP team for the opportunity, not only to read this contribution, but to consider it in depth and reflect on my own thinking through that process.

The first issue I want to consider concerns the methodology that these authors have used to analyse and synthesise the learning from massive amounts of data into a coherent and defensible set of interpretations, in order to address large and

	The Teaching and Learning Research Programme Aims
Learning	To conduct research with the potential to improve outcomes for learners in a very wide range of UK contexts across the lifecourse. To explore synergies between different research approaches and to aim to build UK capacity in conducting high quality educational research. To commit to the application of findings to policy and practice, to work to maximise the impact of the research and to present it in an accessible way.
Outcomes	TLRP studied a broad range of learning outcomes. These included both the acquisition of skill, understanding, knowledge and qualifications and the development of attitudes, values and identities relevant to a learning society.
Lifecourse	TLRP supported research projects on many ages and stages in education, training and lifelong learning. The Programme was concerned with patterns of success and difference, inclusion and exclusion through the lifecourse.
Enrichment	TLRP was committed to engaging users in its work. It worked in all disciplines and sectors of education and used a wide range of appropriate methodology. TLRP cooperated with other researchers within and beyond the UK whenever appropriate.
Expertise	TLRP worked to enhance capacity for all forms of research on teaching and learning, and for research-informed policy and practice.
Improvement	TLRP worked to develop the UK knowledge base on teaching and learning and to make sure that the knowledge it developed was applied in practice and policy

Figure 1. The teaching and learning research programme aims.

important questions about pedagogy and learning and to share their learning broadly. I have entitled it 'Going big and being bold: creating and mobilising knowledge for use'. The second issue, which is close to my own work and resonates for me, is related to Assessment for Learning (AfL) and the research that occurred in the Learning How To Learn (LHTL) project. This one I call 'Getting to the "spirit" of Assessment for Learning'.

Going big and being bold: creating and mobilising knowledge for use

The explosion of knowledge is revolutionising society and escalating the pace of change. Increasingly, managing and distributing knowledge is critical for societal success. Indeed, in 1996, OECD reported that:

> OECD countries continue to evidence a shift from industrial to post-industrial knowledge-based economies. Here, productivity and growth are largely determined by the rate of technical progress and the accumulation of knowledge. Of key importance are networks or systems which can efficiently distribute knowledge and information. (18)

In a world that is increasingly calling for evidence-based decision-making by government and within professions, the task of academic researchers has become more difficult. It is no longer sufficient to do individual academic studies and report them in scholarly journals. If research studies are going to be useful for decisions about policy or practice, the results from academic research need to be organised and contextualised for use by non-researchers.

This need has spawned a whole new field referred to as knowledge transfer, knowledge management or knowledge mobilisation (depending on the context) that has grown from a range of disciplines and has evolved into a distinct field of research and practice. The intention of knowledge mobilisation is to draw from different disciplines that generally do not communicate, resolve competing terms, models and paradigms and aggregate the accumulated knowledge to higher levels so that they can be accessed and utilised across many groups (Moteleb and Woodman 2007). The recognition that it is important for researchers to develop systematic, transparent and defensible processes for synthesising research and making it accessible to others was the motivation for the creation of organisations like the Cochrane Collaboration (medicine) and the Campbell Collaboration (social, behavioural and educational areas) to provide mechanisms for people to make well-informed decisions about the effects of interventions in these areas. These organisations, along with a number of other agencies like the EPPI Centre at the Institute of Education, University of London, and The Best Evidence Synthesis Programme in the New Zealand Ministry of Education, are producing rigorous systematic reviews and syntheses of research literature for use by policymakers and practitioners to ensure that research and the decisions that arise from them are well founded and socially robust Tranfield, Denyer and Smart (2003).

In my own work, I have been grappling with what appears to be the one-way nature of the movement of knowledge in these paradigms, especially in the academic arena. The knowledge management and knowledge mobilisation literature tends to focus on a variety of methods in which research and knowledge is transferred, translated and exchanged to enhance the practical application of knowledge and inform decisions in public policy and professional practice. It is concerned with getting the right information to the right people at the right time in the right format so as to influence decisionmaking (Rock 2009). My dilemma is, 'how does this process of organising and packaging knowledge for easy access fit with the burgeoning knowledge base about how people learn and how they come to accept and integrate new knowledge into their thinking and their practice?' In a recent book chapter, we have tried to explicate some of these issues (Earl and Hannay 2009). We argue that:

> In the knowledge-based society, there is a recognition that knowledge is multi-faceted and can be a tool, a process and a product, all at the same time. Knowledge is infor-

mation that is available for investigation and use (tool) during knowledge creation (process) that results in new understanding and action (product). Knowledge can be viewed as static and immutable information that can be transferred from one person to another with explicit knowledge that was codified as the collective wisdom of the culture and passed on being the most important. When knowledge is conceived as a dynamic and ever-changing commodity that is constructed and tested by individuals as they seek solutions to new problems (Hakkarainen et al. 2004; Hoban 2002), tacit knowledge that is acquired through practical experience (Lam 2000) becomes a critical element in the definition of knowledge as well.

Knowledge work is the process of intentionally combining tacit and explicit knowledge to come to new insights that are distributed across and beyond the organization. When people engage in knowledge work they are actively participating in a cyclical process of new learning and sharing of ideas to stimulate and foster innovative solutions to real problems. This process provides the forum for generation of ideas, challenging assumptions, testing hypotheses, formulating plans and routinely monitoring progress and making adjustments.

The creation of knowledge is not the job of any one individual. It is a social process (Scardamalia and Bereiter 2003) that requires collective responsibility for accomplishments. Knowledge leaders share responsibility for the interrelated network of ideas, sub-goals, and designs, with success dependent on all members rather than concentrated in the leader. As issues emerge, the group works collectively to shape next steps, build on each other's strengths, and improve their ideas and designs. Members create the cultural capital of their organization as they refine the 'knowledge space' and share the learning from their collective work. (186–187)

So, in my thinking, knowledge mobilisation includes aggregation and packaging of explicit knowledge, but it also requires knowledge work – direct and active engagement with the knowledge in ways that make tacit knowledge visible and allow the participants to draw on both tacit and explicit knowledge as they share the learning from their collective work.

As I read James and Pollard's contribution to this volume, I was immediately struck that the TLRP team had moved far beyond knowledge mobilisation as an exercise in aggregation of findings and creative mechanisms for dissemination. Instead, they embedded the creation and sharing of knowledge into the programme in an iterative and intentional way. They constructed the programme, from the beginning, as a process that included ongoing participation in organising, synthesising, understanding and sharing their learning, within their multi-disciplinary team and beyond it through dissemination through a wide range of artefacts and conversations. They have done what I could only imagine.

In the process, James and Pollard have been able to show the complexity, challenge and planning that are necessary to create and mobilise higher-order knowledge through a continuous process running through and alongside the research process, not bolted on when the research is done. As they say:

Individual projects within the Programme focused on different research questions and utilised a range of methods and theoretical resources. Across-programme thematic seminar series and task groups enabled emerging findings to be analysed, synthesised and communicated to wider audiences.

When it comes to creating and sharing knowledge the team has drawn on the knowledge mobilisation literature and they have been true to Principle 3 as it emerged from the multi-layered TLRP analysis – *that effective pedagogy recognises the importance of prior experience and learning*. In their contribution, James and Pollard describe how this process was planned and also how it unfolded to connect the diverse bodies of work through iterative experiences of working collaboratively in order to move beyond the individual studies, to expose and engage with prior learning and experiences, to learn from one another, to organise and reconfigure the learning from the studies and to share the work more broadly. This account also shows how the knowledge work has been constructed to travel beyond the research and move along the knowledge to action continuum to see how this new knowledge could support interventions and innovation.

In my view, this programme provides a high-level example of a major advance in methodology that has been responsive to the complexity of the concepts they were trying to understand. The TLRP provided an initial framework for the group to work under the same umbrella, but it was the commitment of the Directors' team that created the conditions for a 'broad church' interpretation of the data. They moved the programme from a collection of studies to a coherent, robust and valuable new set of principles that are now stimulating the next round of conversations and interventions. In the process, the TLRP team has been true to their own evolving understanding of what makes quality pedagogy and engaged in these practices, as part of their own journeys as new learners – modelling the dialogic approach, and constructing and negotiating meaning by making their own theories and assumptions visible and open for investigation, alongside the empirical evidence.

This process provides a model that can and should be emulated by other researchers: those who are already working in teams and those who are not, but should. The complexity of the learning endeavour is too important to expect single academic studies or even high-quality syntheses of many studies to produce the social capital that will result in productive action. It requires ongoing collaborative interaction with the ideas in ways that elevate the work, to establish new theoretical and pragmatic possibilities.

Getting to the 'spirit' of Assessment for Learning

My second issue is one that is dear to my heart. I have spent much of my academic career investigating what actually happens as teachers engage in assessment in their classrooms (Earl 2003, 2004; Earl and Katz 2003, 2006a, 2008). In particular, I (like many others) have been influenced by the work of the Assessment Reform Group in the United Kingdom and the possibility for classroom assessment to have enormous impact on students' learning. It seemed like one of the most important discoveries in education. Assessment could be at the core of learning. In a book that I wrote in 2003, I argued that assessment actually was learning. I introduced the notion of Assessment *As* Learning to:

> ... reinforce the role of formative assessment by emphasizing the role of the student, not only as a contributor to the assessment and learning process, but the critical connector between them. The student is the link. Students, as active, engaged and critical assessors can make sense of information, relate it to prior knowledge, and master the skills involved. This is the regulatory process in meta-cognition. It occurs when students personally monitor what they are learning and use the feedback from this monitoring to make adjustments, adaptations and even major changes in what they understand. *Assessment as learning* is the ultimate goal, where students are their own best assessors. (Earl 2003, 47)

I have been troubled, however. People did not seem to 'get it'. Even when the book was being used as a text for initial teacher training, formative assessment was being interpreted as having routine assessments throughout a course to track students' progress, without using the assessment to identify misunderstandings and misconceptions or to engage students in thinking about their own learning. Teachers who espoused their belief in AfL used many of the techniques associated with assessment for learning, including peer and self-assessment, but they were mostly being used as mini-assessments that were practice for a final summative assessment. I have seen this pattern time and again in primary schools and in secondary schools, in many different places around the world.

In recent years, I have had the pleasure and privilege to participate in an international invitational assessment seminar focused on Assessment for Learning that has pushed me to move further in my thinking about both the power of assessment for learning and about the need for a theory of action that would move from promise, to action, to impact. This group is made up of researchers, policymakers, professional development providers and educational leaders, all of whom are involved in understanding and promoting high-quality assessment for learning in schools. One of the recurring themes for the group was the same issue that was troubling me. We know that formative assessment, done well, is very powerful:

> Recent reviews of more than 4,000 research investigations show clearly that when this process is well implemented in the classroom, it can essentially double the speed of student learning. Indeed, when one considers several recent reviews of research regarding the classroom formative-assessment process, it is clear that the process works, it can produce whopping gains in students' achievement, and it is sufficiently robust so that different teachers can use it in diverse ways, yet still get great results with their students (Popham 2011).

But, over and over again, we find that the promise of formative assessment is not realised in classrooms. The Learning How to Learn (LHTL) Project within TLRP has provided the international seminar with a major source of evidence and fuelled our deliberations. In their work, the LHTL team found that teachers' implementation of assessment *for* learning in their classrooms often reflected what they called 'the letter' of formative assessment or assessment to promote student autonomy, focusing on the surface techniques, rather than 'the spirit', based on a deep understanding of the principles underlying the practices. These teachers were engaged in practical implementation often based on limited understanding and superficial adoption of the ideas (Black 2007). Only about 20% of the teachers in their Learning How to Learn study were using assessment in ways that were designed to help students to become more independent as learners. They observed that teachers with 'the spirit' did not just add strategies to their existing assessment repertoire; they internalised the underlying principles, had a strong belief in the importance of promoting student autonomy, articulated a clear conviction that they were responsible for ensuring that this took place and took this empowering philosophy into the classroom and communicated it to students in the way they taught (James and Pedder 2006). As James and Pollard describe it in their contribution to the present volume:

> The LHTL project demonstrated that, although advice on specific techniques is useful in the short term, longer-term development and sustainability depends on re-evaluating

beliefs about learning, reviewing the way learning activities are structured, and rethinking classroom roles and relationships.

And therein lies the dilemma. How to move from techniques and activities to genuine new learning by the adults: learning that will change their thinking and their practices? The LHTL project also investigated the conditions in schools and networks that would enable the positive effects of assessment for learning (AfL) to be scaled up and sustained without intensive and expensive support. The researchers found that:

- classroom-focused enquiry by teachers is a key condition of promoting autonomous learning by pupils and that schools that embed AfL make support for professional learning a priority.
- educational networks are much talked about but little understood, and electronic tools for professional development purposes are not well used.
- the intellectual capital of schools can be built on the social capital developed through teachers' personal networking practices (James and Pollard 2011, this volume).

This finding is very resonant with work we have been doing over a number of years investigating the power of networks, learning communities and learning conversations as the venue for the professional learning of adults in schools (Earl and Katz 2006b; Earl and Timperley 2008; Katz, Earl, and Ben Jaafar 2009). Like the LHTL project, we have found that professional communities and networks can offer a powerful venue for building capacity and changing practice in ways that make a difference for student learning. However, these learning communities themselves need to be both focused and intentional to make a difference. Our research has shown that successful learning communities depend on the members of the group engaging in collaborative inquiry. However, collaborative inquiry is not a well-established practice in education and is an important new skill that requires cultivation (Earl and Katz 2006b). Collaborative inquiry involves working together in repeated episodes of reflection and action to examine and learn about an issue that is of importance to the group. When teachers engage in collaborative inquiry, they search for and consider various sources of knowledge (both explicit and tacit) in order to investigate practices and ideas through a number of lenses, to put forward hypotheses, to challenge beliefs, and to pose more questions and to embark on a course of action to address authentic problems (Katz, Earl, and Ben Jaafar 2009). New knowledge can emerge as they come across new ideas or discover that ideas that they believe to be true do not hold up when under scrutiny and this recognition is used as an opportunity to rethink what they know and do (Earl and Timperley 2008). Collaborative inquiry that challenges the status quo enables the kind of professional learning that contributes to changed practice.

When the members of a learning community do not engage in collaborative inquiry, they are not likely to challenge their tacit knowledge. Instead, they attempt to make sense of new ideas by transforming them into something that is already familiar so that they fit with what they already think and believe (Bransford, Brown, and Cocking 1999). But such preservation and conservation – known collectively as *cognitive biases* – make it difficult for people to engage in conceptual change – *real* changes in how and what people think and know that enable them to see the world differently (Katz, Earl, and Ben Jaafar 2009). The misunderstanding about 'assessment for learning' is a classic example of tacit knowledge superseding new knowledge and getting in the way of the kind of conceptual change that is required to truly shift practices so that assessment in the classroom can become the powerful learning force that it has the potential to be. By recognising the natural human propensity to conserve and preserve existing knowledge, it is possible to understand just how difficult 'inquiry' – as a search for deep understanding – truly is. Deep understanding very often means much more than confirming what people think they know; it means *changing* what people think and know. This is the hard work of conceptual change. It means learning to live with the ambiguity and the feeling of dissonance as tacit knowledge and evidence butt heads. And even more than this, it means recognising that this kind of psychological discomfort is a necessary precursor to real new understanding. If AfL is as powerful as the research to date suggests, the challenge is to find ways to use learning communities and networks as vehicles for collaborative inquiry – uncovering existing beliefs and values and introducing the ideas that underpin successful AfL practices in classrooms, so that the participants move beyond the activities to conceptual change.

Learning from TLRP

Both of the issues that I have addressed in this response arise from the same conceptual and practical domain: how to create the conditions for people to make their collective existing conceptions and beliefs visible and examine them along with explicit knowledge in the field, with the potential for conceptual change that will actually influence how they think and behave. This remains one of the most perplexing and challenging areas for investigation and for action. TLRP has offered new images, examples and insights to enhance knowledge in the field and move both theory and practice forward.

References

Black, P. 2007. Formative assessment: Promises or problems? Unpublished paper. http://www.mantleoftheexpert.com/studying/articles/Paul%20Black2007.pdf (accessed March 14, 2010).

Bransford, J.D., A.L. Brown, and R.R. Cocking. 1999. *How people learn: Brain, mind, experience, and school*. Washington, DC: National Academy Press.

Earl, L. 2003. *Assessment as learning: Using classroom assessment to maximise student learning*. Thousand Oaks, CA: Corwin.

Earl, L. 2004. Collecting the evidence: Gathering the right clues. *London Curriculum Bulletin* 2, no. 2: 41.

Earl, L., and S. Katz. 2003. Changing classroom assessment: Teachers' struggles. In *The sharp edge of educational change*, ed. N. Bascia and A. Hargreaves. London: Falmer.

Earl, L., and S. Katz. 2006a. Rethinking classroom assessment with purpose in mind. Western and north curriculum partnership. http://www.wncp.ca/english/subjectarea/class-assessment.aspx (accessed November, 2009).

Earl, L., and S. Katz. 2006b. How networked learning communities work. Centre for Strategic Education Seminar Series Paper No 155. Melbourne.

Earl, L., and S. Katz. 2008. Getting to the core of learning: Using assessment for self-monitoring and self-regulation. In *Unlocking assessment: Understanding for reflection and application*, ed. S. Swaffield, 90–104. London: Routledge/Taylor & Francis.

Earl, L., and L. Hannay. 2009. Evidence based inquiry in support of a knowledge creating school district. Paper presented at the international congress for school effectiveness and school improvement, January 2009, in Vancouver, Canada.

Earl, L., and H. Timperley eds. 2008. *Professional learning conversations: Challenges in using evidence for improvement*. Amsterdam: Springer.

Hakkarainen, K., T. Palonen, S. Paavola, and E. Lehtinen. 2004. *Communities of networked expertise: Professional and educational perspectives*. Amsterdam: Elsevier.

Hoban, G.F. 2002. *Teacher learning for educational change*. Philadelphia: Open University Press.

James, M., and D. Pedder. 2006. Beyond method: Assessment and learning practices and values. *The Curriculum Journal* 17, no. 2: 109–38.

Katz, S., L. Earl, and S. Ben Jaafar. 2009. *Building and connecting learning communities: The power of networks for school improvement*. Thousand Oaks, CA: Corwin.

Lam, A. 2000. Tacit knowledge, organizational learning and societal institutions: An integrated framework. *Organizational Studies* 21, no. 3: 487–513.

Moteleb, A.A., and M. Woodman. 2007. Notions of knowledge management systems: A gap analysis. *The Electronic Journal of Knowledge Management* 5, no. 1: 55–62.

OECD. 1996. *The knowledge-based economy*. Paris: OCDE/GD(96)102.

Popham, J. 2011. Formative assessment – a process, not a test. *Education Week*. http://www.edweek.org/ew/articles/2011/02/23/21popham.h30.html? (accessed February 22, 2011).

Rock, D. 2009. Knowledge broker stories: Defining knowledge mobilization from a strategic perspective. Weblog Entry. Knowledge Mobilization Works Blog. Posted December 7. http://bit.ly/6TntBs (accessed February 26, 2011).

Scardamalia, M., and C. Bereiter. 2003. Knowledge building. In *Encyclopedia of education*. 2nd. ed., 1370–3. New York: Macmillan.

Tranfield, D., D. Denyer, and P. Smart. 2003. Towards a methodology for developing evidence-informed management knowledge by means of systematic review. *British Journal of Management* 14, no. 3: 207–22.

Index